FOR THE LOVE OF ANN

James Copeland is 35. He is Deputy Northern Editor of the *Sunday People*. Born in Kilmarnock, Scotland, he started his career as a journalist in Glasgow. He worked variously as a reporter, feature-writer and sub-editor on several Scottish papers before joining the *Sun* in Manchester in 1964. He later moved to the *Daily Mirror* and was appointed to his present post in 1971. Married, he lives with his wife and two daughters in a rambling Victorian house in Bury, Lancashire.

FOR THE
LOVE
OF ANN

Based on a diary by Jack Hodges

by
James Copeland

BALLANTINE BOOKS • NEW YORK

© James Copeland 1973

All rights reserved under International and
Pan-American Copyright Conventions.

SBN 345-25089-3

This edition published by arrangement with
Arrow Books, Ltd.

First printing: March, 1974

First special printing: November, 1975

Cover painting by Gary Watson

Printed in the United States of America

BALLANTINE BOOKS
A Division of Random House, Inc.
201 East 50th Street, New York, N.Y. 10022

Contents

Acknowledgements

I wish to place on record my sincere thanks to the many pople who helped make this book possible, but especially to:

Dr. Lorna Wing, M.D., D.P.M., a member of the advisory panel for the National Society for Autistic Children, for her patience in teaching me so much about autism;

Mr. George Glover for giving up so much of his valuable time to explain his teaching methods;

Mr. Robert Edwards, Editor of the *Sunday People* when the story of Ann was published in that paper, and now Editor of the *Sunday Mirror;* and Mr. Alan Hobday, Northern Editor of the *Sunday People,* for their encouragement.

J.C.

For all the Anns and their parents

Preface

The counsulting room was long and narrow, with a high-vaulted ceiling. It was at the end of a narrow, echoing corridor in the hospital.

From the windows one could look out on the Autumn-tinted trees, and in the silence of that room it was hard to realise that only a few hundred yards away was the bustling life of industrial Manchester.

There were four people in the room on that chill September day. The doctor sat behind his desk reading a report. Facing him was a young couple, hardly daring to breathe as he studied the papers in front of him.

The silence in the room was broken only by the constant rocking of the little girl sitting in a chair by their side. To and fro she went. Monotonously. Her large blue eyes staring—yet taking nothing in. A lovely child with a peaches and cream complexion. Her brown-blond hair peeped out in plaits from her blue bonnet.

The doctor cleared his throat and spoke very quietly. "I am so very sorry to have to tell you this, but I'm afraid that our tests show that it is extremely unlikely that your daughter will ever be educated, or for that matter, that she will ever be able to recognise you as her parents."

Jack and Ivy Hodges looked at each other and a chill

gripped their hearts as the words sank in. Ivy's eyes filled with tears, but she managed to fight back the sobs. She wanted to cry out and she felt as though she were about to choke. Her head swam.

After a few more formalities, they were shown out of the room by the sympathetic doctor and they stumbled their way along the corridor.

They made no attempt to hold the little girl's hand, knowing that to do so would release a snarling, spitting, screaming animal. The child whimpered as Ivy's shoe heels clicked on the polished floor and down the twenty-six marble steps—and out into the weak sunshine.

The couple walked in silence down the long, sweeping drive. Too numbed to talk. They ignored the waiting bus and instead turned down the road to walk the seemingly endless five miles to their home in Salford. Buses and taxis were out of the question. To have attempted to use one would have started the screaming again. Instead they guided the little girl by touching her shoulder whenever she was in danger of walking into the road. It was almost an automatic action by now. They had become so used to it over the years.

That was in 1958 and Ann Hodges was six years and eight months old. In the words of the doctor she was a schizophrenic and a psychopath.

To Jack and Ivy she was simply a walking vegetable. A beautiful child—incredibly so—wrapped up in her own world. Oblivious to all human contact. Impervious to sights of beauty and sounds of joy.

Today that same girl is in her twenties. Full of chat

and charm. Devoted to her parents and her brothers and excitedly taking in the world and its challenges.

Between those two dates lies a remarkable story. A love story born out of hopelessness and ignorance and nurtured in years of tears and joy.

For by the time Jack and Ivy Hodges reached their house that day they had made up their minds on two very important issues.

Ann would NOT be committed to a mental home as the doctor had suggested, and they refused point-blank to accept that she was incurable.

To them, a child as beautiful as Ann could NOT be a mental defective. It didn't add up. It didn't make sense. Mental defectives had that certain look about them, was how they put it.

What they didn't know then, and were not to learn for many years, was that Ann was autistic. The word had been coined a few years before from the Greek for "self." It describes in one poignant word those children who cannot communicate with the outside world, although in many cases they have perfect brains, sight and hearing.

The word is comparatively new, but experts generally agree that there must always have been autistic children. In fact, one of the best descriptions was written at the end of the eighteenth century by a French physician, Dr. Itard, who looked after and taught a boy who behaved in this strange fashion. His book *Wild Boy of Aveyron*, describing his teaching methods, received scant attention at the time. It is now accepted by twentieth-century experts as a classic description of autism.

But it was not until the 1940s that an American psychiatrist, Leo Kanner, pin-pointed the fact that there was a definite group of children who had these strange behaviour patterns. He called it "early childhood autism".

It is now known that at least four or five children in every 10,000 are affected; that there are three or four autistic boys to every autistic girl. It has also been established that the problems are present from birth, or begin within the first two or three years, and that the parents of these children tend to be above average intelligence.

All that is known. But no one knows the cause for certain. There may be many things that can lead to the same condition, but most experts agree that the main problem lies in the functioning of the brain— particularly the parts which deal with information coming from the senses, and the parts which are concerned with language development.

Some believe the problems are due to very slow growth of these parts of the brain, and improvement occurs in later childhood.

However, it seems likely that in some cases the relevant parts of the brain are actually damaged (perhaps by severe infection or some form of shock) and the handicaps are more acute and longer lasting.

Whatever the cause, autistic children behave as if they cannot make sense of the things they see and the things they hear.

In particular they do not understand language. They are in a much worse plight than deaf children, because not only do they not understand the spoken word, they also do not comprehend gestures, facial expressions, miming or information conveyed in pictures.

It is easy to imagine how muddled and frightened an autistic child must be when he hears and sees other people making what to him are strange noises and strange movements, and when everything that happens is completely unpredictable.

The children cannot learn social, practical or academic skills and so remain babyish and difficult. Sometimes, as was to prove in Ann's case, they are so petrified with fear of the world they cannot understand that they learn nothing at all, and close themselves inside a little artificial environment which they try to keep from changing in any way at all.

Today wih modern knowledge of autism, more children are being diagnosed early and proper methods of management and teaching, based on a knowledge of the child's handicaps, are being used from the start. Some of the secondary problems can be avoided by a structured and consistent approach.

The handicaps of early childhood autism can occur in children who are basically of normal, or above normal intelligence. Many, however, are below average in intelligence and therefore the final result of teaching varies a great deal, depending upon the severity of each child's handicaps.

In the early years it is difficult to tell which child will do well and which child will make only a small amount of progress. It is now recognised that it is of vital importance to give every child the best chance possible in education to achieve his maximum potential.

The National Society for Autistic Children (a society for parents and professional workers) now has its own schools and works constantly to bring the children's needs to the attention of the local authorities, many of whom have now started their own special schools.

But in 1958 all this was little known, and completely foreign to Jack and Ivy. The help they so desperately needed was not to come for many years.

Before they cried themselves to sleep that September night they made a pact. No matter what happened they would never give up trying to find a way through to their daughter. No one was going to take her away from them. Even if it took the rest of their lives they would never give up the fight.

They also decided to start a record of everything she did, in the faint hope that it would give them a clue to her troubled mind. The very next day Jack started to write down all he could remember about Ann from the day she was born. Over the years, on scraps of paper and old exercise books—eventually to be transferred to a ledger—he has noted the joys, the sorrows—and the final triumph.

All for the love of Ann. . . .

A Child is Born

Mayor Street, Salford, was narrow and ugly. The houses all had a drab uniformity that made each indistinguishable from its neighbour. They were the worst reminders of the industrial revolution where family crowded on family. In each of those dozens of identical streets men, women and children had lived, loved and died for generations. It was the area that became Walter Greenwood's Hankey Park in *Love on the Dole*.

To Jack and Ivy Hodges No. 28 was far from the ideal home they had dreamed of when they married in 1947, but it was a palace compared to the flat in which they had started married life. Besides, with the war just over they were thankful to at least have a place they could call their own. Jack brought paint and paper and they soon had the little two-up, two-down house gleaming. All they wanted now was to settle down and bring up a family.

For Jack, so recently out of the Army, Mayor Street was a haven of peace. He had survived the horrors of the Italian campaign and nothing could upset him now. They were both Salford born and bred and they had witnessed the appalling effects of poverty. Jack's own father had been on the dole throughout the hungry thirties and he was determined that the same thing would not happen to him.

7

He was an enginner and with the country beginning to boom again he was in full employment. Life at No. 28 Mayor Street was good.

In October 1950, Ivy presented him with a son. They christened him Leonard and he became the apple of their eye. They both loved children and often discussed what size family they should have. They would like two boys and two girls.

And so on a bitterly cold day, on January 10, 1952, the girl that was to change the course of their lives was born at No. 28 Mayor Street.

As Ivy's time drew near Jack was ushered out of the house by fussing neighbours and the midwife to kick his heels for the next couple of hours at his mother's home in the next street. When he was told that the baby was born he rushed over the frosted pavements to gaze at his daughter. She weighed seven and a half pounds and was completely bald. But as Jack gazed down at her he felt that he was looking at a beauty queen.

The birth had been uneventful, but one incident that morning was to torment them in the harrowing years that followed.

While the midwife was attending to Ivy she left the baby on the end of the bed without any covering. In the to-ing and fro-ing someone left the street door open. Within minutes the baby was thoroughly chilled —"blue with cold" one of the fussing women said. When Jack arrived Ivy was in tears and neighbours were smearing the baby with olive oil and wrapping her up in warm blankets.

The incident was soon over and Jack felt he could

safely leave the house, gather up a few friends and announce the baby's arrival in the traditional fashion at the local pub.

His heart was singing. He had a home of his own, a wonderful wife and two lovely children. Although work was hard and he had to put in long and exhausting hours he felt that life was good and he was determined to improve his little family's lot in every way he could.

Ann was a good baby. An exceptionally good baby. She cried when she was hungry—and that was all. As the weeks rolled by EVERYONE remarked on just how good she was. She would lie in her pram for hours at a time and it was easy to forget she was even there. She was developing perfectly, took all her feed and was putting on weight at a normal rate. But she appeared to take very little interest in the things around her.

However, Jack and Ivy weren't too worried to begin with. They just thanked their lucky stars that they had been blessed with such a good baby.

Her hair was growing—a golden blonde—and they decided to let it grow until it was long enough to plait. They loved little girls with long hair and they knew how the other little girls in the street loved their long tresses. They spent hours discussing what sort of dresses they would buy her when she was walking. They talked of dolls and prams—and of little girls growing up.

But as the weeks rolled on the niggling doubts began. Ann didn't gurgle and coo like other babies. She didn't make a sound except when she was hungry.

Now she was sitting up by herself and yet not once did she put out her arms to be picked up and cuddled. Nothing. She showed no recognition.

Nights became alarming experiences. She would lie staring fixedly at the light above her cot for hours on end. Jack decided to fix a paper shield over the light. But as soon as he did that Ann started to cry. No tears. Just a dry crying sound that eventually turned into a horrifying scream, and the shade had to be removed to get some respite.

Jack and Ivy Hodges had been subjected to the first bout of screaming that was to become part of their daily lives for the next fourteen years.

By the time Ann was six months old it was obvious that she resented anyone picking her up. When Ivy took her out of her pram to get her ready for bed the crying and screaming would start and continue though bathtime until the baby was back in her cot —and staring at the light.

Those first niggling doubts were taking on an aura of horror. No matter what time of night they went in to her, she appeared to be awake—staring at that light. Weaning her was also proving virtually impossible. Every time they tried to spoon-feed her she screamed until they gave her back the bottle. One particular bottle and teat. She would entertain no other.

But after months of heartbreaking effort, they scored a minor victory.

They managed to get her to suck semi-solids from a spoon. But only by giving her the bottle to suck between mouthfuls. Each mealtime became a marathon mind-shattering experience for Jack and Ivy. The bottle had become the child's centre of affection. Part of her very life. It went everywhere with her. And that bottle—eventually nicknamed "dolly" by the family—was to be part and parcel of Ann's life until she was seven years old.

By the time she was ten months, Ann was showing signs of walking and Jack and Ivy began to breathe more easily. At least there was nothing wrong with her limbs and, anyway, perhaps she would soon get out of these tantrums.

But it was impossible not to compare her to Leonard. He was a strapping little boy, full of fun, chat and mischief. A loving child who would throw his arms round his parents for a hug and a cuddle and prattle away to them. Ann would sit wide-eyed, seemingly unseeing and uncaring.

Now her walking was bringing unmentionable fears. She had boundless energy and would run around the house for hours on end, bumping into furniture, falling and fumbling—and never showing any sign of hurt or pain. If anyone tried to pick her up she would start those piercing screams and fight to get away.

But worst of all she made no attempt to talk or communicate in any way.

Heartbroken Jack and Ivy went to see their doctor. He admitted he was puzzled. But the child seemed normal in every respect and he told them to be patient. She would probably grow out of it, he said. The couple were far from happy. They had seen countless children grow up, but they had never seen one behave the way their daughter was doing. There was now no doubt in their minds that all was far from well. But what?

They persevered. They struggled and tried to cope with something that neither of them could understand. A gnawing horror was hammering at their minds but close as they were, they were too afraid to talk about it.

Then Ivy was pregnant again. Through her confinement she still tried to get through to her angelic-looking daughter. But it was in vain. When Leslie was born in October 1953, Ann was twenty months old. She had not uttered one word or shown any sign of recognition in that time.

The new baby brought a ray of happiness to Jack and Ivy. They were on the last lap of their ideal family. But it was not to be. The bouts of screaming were becoming more and more frequent and life was becoming unbearable for the young couple. Then fate dealt them a further blow. Ivy's mother—their staunch ally and friend, their greatest help—was injured in a road accident. They spent sleepless nights at the hospital, but after a few days she died.

It was as though a light had gone out in their lives. She had been such a marvellous woman. She had helped share the growing, secret burden. She had lifted their spirits when they were down. Now she was no more. They were, to all intents, on their own. True, their neighbours were wonderful. But if Jack and Ivy couldn't understand their daughter, it was impossible for strangers to do so.

By now her behaviour was beyond all reason. She had become obsessed with a chair—one particular chair—and would sit for hours rocking to and fro in it. Then she would bang her head against the wall, and scream if anyone tried to stop her. She pulled her hair out in handfuls and stuffed it in her mouth.

The district nurse who came to visit Ivy after Leslie was born became very concerned about the little girl and suggested that they should take her to see a specialist. He admitted he was baffled and sent them on a round of other specialists. Her ears were examined, her eyes, her arms and legs and her chest. But no one could come up with a reason for her behaviour.

They trudged from hospital to hospital, from doctor to doctor. It went on for month after weary month. And it was brought to a halt—by a dog.

As they walked along the street on their way from another fruitless consultation, a large dog ran over to Ann. She stood still in the middle of the street—and screamed. The screams became even more terrible when Jack tried to pick her up. That day she screamed for sixteen hours, and only stopped when she fell asleep from sheer exhaustion.

So they became prisoners in their own home. They could only go out one at a time with the boys. If they tried to take Ann out, the screams would start again.

Then one day they tried sitting her in the pram with the hood up. They gave her "dolly" to suck and she went out without a murmur. But even that brought its own troubles. The pram became an obsession, and the screams would start when they lifted her out. So another problem had to be solved. Eventually, they found that by letting her stay in the pram they could get some peace and quiet.

So every night they carried Ann in the pram up

the little narrow staircase in Mayor Street, and every morning they carried her down in it.

There were the occasional days of comparative calm, with hardly a sound from the little girl. But they were few and far between. In truth, the screaming was gaining in length and intensity.

And on one dreadful, never-to-be-forgotten night of horror the screams became so bad that a passing policeman burst into the house convinced the child was being attacked. The distraught and tearful couple did their best to explain to him about their daughter. But the shame they felt that night was something they were never to forget.

Their nerves were shattered through worry and lack of sleep. Rows blew up over the tiniest things as they tried to find a way out of the nightmare that was engulfing them—and they foundered. But somehow they found the strength to go on.

Jack was working night-shift and would arrive home at 8:15 a.m. in time to take over from Ivy who had been up most of the night trying to cope with the increasing impossibility of a child who could not, or would not, co-operate in any way. Ivy would go to bed until 1 p.m. and then get up to let Jack have some rest before he had to go back on night-shift.

And so the endless days grew into months—and slowly into years. They lived their lives wrapped only in their little family and restricted by the walls of their tiny house. They only left it for the bare essentials of life . . . Jack to go to work and Ivy to do the necessary shopping.

When Ann was three-and-a-half, they took stock. And it made a very dismal picture for the couple.

This child of the long, blonde hair, the almost angelically beautiful features and the large, blue eyes was a complete stranger to them.

They left her alone with her obsession for rocking, they gave up trying to teach her personal cleanliness. They forced food into her and at night they dosed her with aspirin in a heartbreaking attempt to get away from the screams that pervaded their very existence.

They hated what they were doing, but they had to find some peace, if not for themselves, then for the boys who were growing rapidly and were completely bewildered by the snarling, spitting animal that was their sister.

They had soon given up trying to play with her. She was vicious and destructive with any toy they gave her. All she wanted were pieces of string, sticks and stones and to be left alone rocking in her chair. And always at hand was "dolly."

The teat had now grown to obscene proportions through constant sucking and being scalded with boiling water.

Jack and Ivy tried to change it for a new one, but Ann was not deceived. In a way it was uncanny. Here was a child showing every sign of being mentally subnormal, but she could immediately tell if the teat had been changed, even though Jack had spent hours doctoring a new one to look like the old.

Clothes and shoes were now becoming a problem. It took weeks of perserverance to get her to put on anything new. Ann would scream and try to tear them off. Eventually they found a way round it by letting her wear her old clothes on alternate days, until she became obsessed with the new clothes.

Ivy, who had dreamed for so long of dressing her little daughter up in bows and frills, grew to dread the days when the child required anything new at all. Ann hated change of any kind—including new wallpaper. When Jack re-papered their little lounge, Ann screamed for three days.

One day when Ivy was out shopping she saw a bonnet in a shop. It was pale blue, with long silk ribbons. It was made for a little girl. It was the kind of bonnet a little girl would love and cherish. It was expensive—a bit more than they could afford, really. But Ivy went ahead and bought it. It was just the sort of thing that Ann could so easily become attached to. Ivy rushed home with it, and despite protests put it on Ann's head.

In the appalling screaming fit that followed Ann tore the bonnet from her head and ripped it to shreds. Ivy, not for the first time in her life, was reduced to bitter tears.

They were now giving up any hope of rearing her like a normal human being. They catered for her basic needs and left it at that. For her part, Ann would not entertain animation of any kind—whether it was humans, dogs, cats or any animal, or even any toy that resembled them.

In their bewilderment, the couple tramped once again from doctor to doctor and clinic to clinic. But although everyone was sympathetic, no one could give them any helpful advice.

When she was four years old, Ann was sent to a child guidance clinic for an IQ test, which was a hopeless failure. In fact, Jack and Ivy were not to learn for many years that she had registered nothing at all, and the staff had been too upset to tell them.

But at least the clinic began to take an interest in the little girl and Jack and Ivy were called for an interview by one of the doctors. He questioned them about their health, their background and anything they could think of about Ann.

After several interviews like this, the doctor told Jack and Ivy that he thought Ann was suffering from "an emotional disturbance of the mind." Her mind, he told them, was as though it were wrapped in a thick fog which would not clear. She would not entertain anything she could not understand. But he was reluctant to venture an opinion as to whether or not she could be cured. So little was known about the condition, he told them, that there was no point in raising false hopes in their minds. But he felt that a brain X-ray would at least establish whether or not there was abnormality.

For the first time since Ann had started showing her peculiarities, Jack and Ivy felt almost elated. After struggling for so long in the dark on their own, here, at last, was someone who showed a genuine interest in their daughter.

Ann was five now and all around them in Mayor Street other children of her age were starting to go to school. Jack and Ivy would watch them as they chattered their way down the pavement hand-in-hand, satchels on their backs. Sometimes the couple would stand at their door and watch little girls at play—taking their dolls for walks to the pocket-handkerchief of a park at the end of the street, or skipping, or playing the street games that had been handed down from mother to daughter for generations.

And Ann would sit in her chair, rocking to and fro sucking "dolly" and staring with vacant eyes at nothing in particular.

It was at moments like this that Jack and Ivy found life very hard to bear. Life had dealt them one of the cruellest blows of all. If Ann had been deformed, or obviously mentally retarded, they felt it would have been somehow easier to bear. But to look at her as she was filled them with despair.

But for the sake of the boys they knew they had to carry on. Life had to be lived each day. Many years later, Jack and Ivy were to admit that there were times when the feeling to run away from it all was so great they had to force themselves to carry on.

Ann was five-and-a-half when Jack and Ivy finally decided they must have a holiday. Since the day she was born they had never gone further than walking distance from Mayor Street. Jack wrote to a boarding house in Blackpool and tried to explain in the letter about Ann's "peculiarities."

There was great excitement when they received a reply saying that the family would be most welcome, and that Ann would be no problem. Now they had to overcome the question of transport for Ann. She was still taken everywhere in her pram with the hood up. Ivy swapped it for a folding trolley—with a hood —and many sleepless nights followed trying to persuade Ann to get into it. But eventually, as with most other things, she accepted it, and indeed, as was her

wont, became obsessed with it. They also bought her
a little upholstered chair which meant that she could
sit out at the front door on fine days rocking, and
sucking her bottle.

By now she had begun to pull strange faces at
nothing at all. Sometimes she would suddenly burst
into peals of laughter and what appeared to be
squeals of delight. The first time it happened, Ivy
was overjoyed and rushed forward to hug her. But the
laughter immediately turned to screams. The laughter
had signified nothing whatsoever. And so once again
they left her on her own whenever possible.

Soon the day arrived for the great adventure—
their holiday by the sea.

When they awoke that morning, the rain was beat-
ing a tattoo on the pavement and they had to walk
half-a-mile to the bus depot. Ann was put in the trolley with Leslie, and Jack picked up the bulging suit-
cases, and off they set. By the time they arrived at
the bus station, they were soaked to the skin and
feeling pretty miserable.

Jack went to the back of the coach to help load the
luggage and Ivy put the boys on the coach. But as
soon as Ann was taken out of the trolley she took one
look at the bus—and was off. Ivy screamed and
Jack ran round in time to see the little girl running like
a hare along the busy, rain-soaked pavement. Traffic
was flowing thick and fast along the road, but the
little girl was completely oblivious to it.

Jack, his heart pumping as though it would burst,
realised he could not get to his daughter before she
reached a road junction a few yards ahead. He

shouted like a madman, but anyone who noticed just stared at him. No one tried to stop the panic-stricken child.

Then she tripped and fell—full-length into a puddle. Jack picked her up and despite her screams hugged her and kissed her and carried her back to the coach.

The noise was appalling and the couple felt that all eyes were on them. But then the screaming stopped as abruptly as it had started and when they sat Ann on the back seat and gave her "dolly" she started rocking in silence.

An old man sitting at the front of the coach walked up to the little girl and handed her a cough sweet. Ann snatched it from his hand, put it to her nose and sniffed it . . . and threw it at the old man. He walked away after telling the couple that their daughter needed a smack for her bad manners. But the couple were staring at Ann, so overcome with amazement that they didn't even try to explain her behaviour.

For the first time in her life, Ann had communicated her dislike for something edible by using her sense of smell. Until that moment she had eaten any food she was given. Ivy took some chocolate from her bag and offered a piece to Ann. And once again she put it to her nose, sniffed it, but this time put it in her mouth. From that day on, and for several years, Ann would sniff her food before deciding to eat it, or reject it.

The rest of the journey was uneventful and the coach was soon in Blackpool. Rain was still falling heavily when they arrived at the Lancashire resort and a cold wind was blowing from the sea. The boarding house was two miles from the bus station and too far for the children to walk. They couldn't face the idea of getting Ann onto another bus or even a taxi. They stood on the pavement—a little bedraggled family group—when a horse-drawn landau pulled up. These neat outfits have been a tourist attraction at the resort for years, and before Ann could bat an eye-lid, Jack picked her up and put her on board, followed by Ivy and the boys. To their amazement Ann didn't offer any protest. The landau, packed with cases and buckets and spades and the family, clopped its way to the boarding house. Muldoon's picnic they called it that day. And Muldoon's picnic they still call it when they remember that eventful holiday.

Their landlady was a charming middle-aged woman with a warm smile who, in her eagerness to show that she thought the little girl perfectly normal, bent down and picked her up. Jack just managed to grab "dolly" as it fell from Ann's hands which were now occupied in trying to scratch the woman. Screams rent the air and the little girl was hurriedly put down again.

Once again, the couple found themselves having to try and explain something they couldn't understand themselves. However, soon all was calm again, but during the rest of the holiday they were aware of the landlady giving Ann some very long, searching looks. But she went out of her way to make the couple and the boys feel at ease. She arranged for them to have a little private dining-room to prevent Jack and Ivy being embarrassed by Ann's peculiar table manners.

The following morning was bright and sunny and so after breakfast they set off for the beach. The boys skipped along with their buckets and spades and Ann sat in the trolley sucking "dolly."

When they arrived at the glorious, golden beach Ann would have nothing to do with it. They took her out of the trolley and tried to get her to walk on the sand, but she just screamed. So they had to put her back in the trolley and carry her that way. They bought her a toy windmill—and she tore it to pieces. For the rest of that day and the following day they just let her sit in the trolley, with her bottle hanging from her mouth.

Then on the third day, something happened that was to prove one of the most significant factors in finding the key to Ann's mind, but Jack and Ivy didn't realise it at the time. In fact, when it happened they thought they were faced with a disaster.

The boys were building sand-castles and Jack and Ivy were stretched out in deck-chairs soaking up the sun. Ann was in her trolley as usual. But she had started to rock to and fro and slowly—before anyone realised what was happening—the trolley tipped over, and threw Ann onto the sand. She landed on her face, scrambled up screaming terribly and ran. She fell again, got up and ran. The screams were horrific as she tried to get away from that sand. But she couldn't. It was all around her. Jack picked her up and put her back into the trolley, and the screams eventually subsided.

Half-an-hour later Jack and Ivy stared in amazement as Ann jumped out of the trolley onto the sand and gave a shout of delight as she picked up a handful of it and held it to her nose and then threw it down.

So, for the rest of that day—and indeed for the rest

of the holiday—she spent her time running around in the sand scooping up great handfuls, with "dolly" hanging from her mouth.

To an outsider it would not seem like very much, but Jack and Ivy had a feeling of elation. In the space of one week, Ann had shown two—albeit tiny—forms of recognition. First with the sweet and then with the sand.

The rest of the holiday passed quickly, and suddenly all too soon, it was time to go home to Mayor Street. They once again hired a landau to take them to the coach station and there were the inevitable screams from Ann when they made her get on the coach, but apart from that it was an uneventful journey.

For some reason they thought that Ann would have forgotten everything in the house. But she ran in and immediately sat on her little chair and started rocking again.

There was a letter waiting for Jack and Ivy from the hospital doctor asking them to call and see him. They tried to curb a rising feeling of hope that he had good news for them. Besides, they were anxious to tell him of what they considered to be Ann's progress.

By now the trolley was beginning to be something of a problem. Ann was too big for it. But for a while they didn't know what to do about it.

Then Ivy swapped it for an older one—without a hood. And to their joy Ann rejected it completely. She refused to sit in it, or have anything to do with it. But strangely there were no screams, no tantrums— except when Ivy tried to pick her up and love her. This was progress indeed. Ann had actually been broken of one of her obsessions without an hysterical outburst.

When they arrived at the hospital the following week, they told the doctor about all the wonderful things Ann had done. He took her into a little room and showed her a sandpit complete with toys. Ann gave a gurgle of pleasure but ignored the toys and picked up a handful of sand and sniffed it.

The doctor told the couple they were deluding themselves. In his opinion, Ann hadn't made any actual progress since he had last seen her. He was gentle, but he was firm. Incidents like the sweet episode and the sand were of no consequence in Ann's development. As her parents, they believed such things were progress because they were willing Ann to be normal.

In all, it was a pretty depressing interview, and it wasn't helped by the fact that the doctor had called them purely to have Ann's head X-rayed. Something that was to prove impossible. She wouldn't sit or lie still. She screamed and clawed at anyone who tried to hold her. After half-an-hour of trying everyone agreed that it was futile.

So it was back home to the old routine. Living each day in their close little world in the house in Mayor Street. And they felt within their hearts when they looked at their daughter, she hadn't made any progress at all. The outlook was bleak indeed. Jack and Ivy were now sure that they would have to cater for Ann's every need for the rest of their lives.

Then a few weeks later they had a visit from a man for the Corporation Housing Department. The couple had been on the waiting list from the day they married in 1947, and now there was a house available for them. It was on the outskirts of the city. It was on the very edge of the green belt. It was surrounded by trees and good fresh air—and they made up their minds to go.

They were going to leave Mayor Street.

The End of "Dolly"

It was not an easy decision to make. Mayor Street had been so much part of their life. Even after they had finally decided to go, they spent many hours into the night talking of all the people and things they would miss in that little community. Here neighbours' doors were always open. True, at the new house they would have a garden and there would be equal opportunity to get to know their new neighbours. But unless you were brought up in a street like Mayor Street it was impossible to really know the spirit of comradeship that environment sponsored. It was like no other.

So when they finally moved, it was with very mixed feelings. They knew they were doing right for their sons. For Ann's part they were sure it wouldn't matter where they went. For her there could be none of the great excitement, none of the feeling of an enormous adventure. Her world was her chair . . . and "dolly." Always "dolly."

They took with them a lot of memories of that little house that had been their fortress and their prison. (Mayor Street as they knew it then no longer exists. In place of all those grubby little houses are fine new buildings. But to this day, and for the rest of their lives, Jack and Ivy Hodges remember Mayor Street with a deep affection.)

On removal day Jack took the boys with him in

the furniture van while Ivy had to walk with Ann, not holding her hand but guiding her along with prods in the back like some dumb animal. They had tried desperately hard to get her to hold hands, but it was no use. It just produced those screams. Jack and Ivy faced the inevitable fact. Ann, far from improving, was getting worse. And as she grew, so did her strength. Moving her from one place to another was an enormous, mind-snapping task.

When Jack and the boys arrived at the new house they helped to move the furniture in, and then Jack made a pot of tea . . . and waited for Ivy and Ann. He knew they had arrived long before he could see them. Those now familiar, dreaded screams echoed through the quiet, tree-lined streets of their new neighbourhood. At least the neighbours weren't going to be left in any doubt as to Ann's capabilities for making a lot of noise. What had started the screams, they were to discover later, was the sight of trees and acres of fresh grass. To the child, surrounded all her short life by brick and concrete, those nodding trees and that rippling grass were objects of terror.

That day is one that will never be forgotten by the family. In a way it marked the lowest ebb in their dealings with their daughter. Perhaps in a way it was the beginning of her fight for a new life. No one will ever be sure. But what is sure is that the day of excitement, the start of a new chapter, ended in bitter tears.

When they got Ann into the house they sat her in her chair and gave her "dolly." But it was no use. The screams wouldn't stop. They got louder and more intense. At one point Ivy found herself in her new

kitchen, her hands over her ears, trying to shut out
those waves of sound. The boys, overawed for a start
by their new surroundings, were tired and tearful.
They had seen their sister like this before, but never
so bad. They were afraid to be in the house with her
as she made that dreadful sound over and over.

Jack, driven to the very depths of distraction, put
up their little tent in the back garden and Leonard
and Leslie Hodges spent the first night at their new
home . . . under canvas.

By now Ann appeared to have gone berserk. She
was rocking in her chair, wailing and screaming.
There were no tears, of course. There never were.
Jack snatched her up and ignoring the punching and
kicking carried her upstairs, still screaming, and
dumped her in the small, empty bedroom and locked
the door.

For the next hour Ann threw herself about on the
floor and screamed. It was as though a tortured
soul was loose. Jack and Ivy shut themselves in the
kitchen—the furthest point from that room—and tried
to shut their ears and their minds to what was happening above them.

Then silence. Sweet peace. Jack and Ivy went quietly upstairs and opened the bedroom door. Ann was
unconscious on the floor. In the midst of her fit she
had banged her head so hard against the wall she had
laid herself out.

Jack Hodges, a man of gentle disposition and a
loving father, went down on his knees by her side . . .
and wept. Gently he picked the little limp bundle
from the floor and carried her downstairs. Ivy, blinded
by tears, gently caressed the child who would not

let her touch her at any other time. Jack rushed from the house to a phone box and called the doctor, but by the time he arrived Ann had come round and a large bruise on her forehead was the only sign that anything had happened to her.

Strangely enough she didn't scream again for two days. It was as though she had spent all her energy in one huge orgy of hysterics. But soon she was back to her usual routine of fighting them every time they tried to feed her or help her in any way.

Jack and Ivy were to wonder for a long time about the rights and wrongs of leaving the child on her own in that little room. They had been driven to it, and they would not willingly harm a hair on her head. In the weeks after that terrible night they were very careful not to do anything that would send Ann into one of those rages. That was a lot easier said than done, of course, because they were never fully sure about WHAT caused that dreadful screaming. It sometimes appeared to them that the smallest thing would bring it on. Sometimes nothing at all.

It was only their deep love for each other and their faith in their children that prevented them from losing their sanity. They knew that the specialists they had seen were interested in Ann, but they realised equally well that those same specialists were baffled. They were for the most part overworked and dedicated men. But they had to give priority to the children who had symptoms they could recognise and perhaps cure. Jack and Ivy realised this and they did not resent it. Whatever was wrong with their daughter was very rare indeed. But they could not help themselves from thinking "someday, someday . . ."

However, there was one bright spot in the next few weeks of misery as Ann's screaming bouts became more frequent and longer. Just when they had reached the point where they were sure they could not take any more they made a startling discovery.

It became obvious that Ann did not scream nearly so much when the curtains were drawn. Then she would sit contentedly in her chair, sucking "dolly." So one morning instead of opening the curtains, Ivy left them drawn—and the light on. Ann was with her. But this time she did not start her screaming. Instead she went straight to her chair and sat down. Suddenly Ivy pulled the curtains back and the effect was startling—and shattering. Ann put her hands over her eyes and screamed. Ivy immediately closed the curtains—and the screaming stopped.

Outside the window was a tall privet bush which swayed in the wind. Ivy was now sure that it was the object of Ann's terror. She explained her theory to Jack when he returned from work and he immediately went outside and chopped the bush down. They then tried the curtain experiment with Ann, and when they were opened this time there were no screams as she looked out of the window.

In fact, from that day she seemed more settled and appeared to at last have accepted her new home. Jack and Ivy were quietly excited. By careful observation they had discovered one of her fears and removed it. Now, they reasoned, if they watched her carefully perhaps they could remove other fears. It would be a mammoth task. But it would certainly be worth trying. Anything would be worth trying.

They were now convinced that somehow, for some

inexplicable reason, Ann did not see and hear the outside world the way they did. Things that other people accepted as normal appeared to hold great terrors for that pathetic little girl. If only . . . If. How many times they repeated that little word.

The house was now looking very much like home. Ivy made new curtains and Jack painted and papered the rooms, which brought the familiar screaming attacks from Ann, but they did their best to ignore her and let her scream it out.

As the weeks grew into months they were regularly attending the hospital clinic with Ann for examinations, most of which proved impossible to carry out. The child appeared to register nothing. Then came that September day when they were told that she was a schizophrenic and psychopath. The doctor was extremely kind and sympathetic. He could help them get Ann into a home, if they wished. Jack and Ivy were having none of it.

After they made their pledge to do all they could to find a way through to Ann a sort of determined peace came over them. Tiredness seemed to vanish and they found they were not having nearly so many rows as before. They were completely united in their pact.

They also realised with a feeling of guilt that so much time was being devoted to Ann that in many ways their now growing sons were being left out of things. So Jack bought fishing tackle for Leonard, Leslie and himself and they spent many happy hours on the river bank. He took them for long walks through the woods and pointed out the beauty of nature. Of course, they couldn't go as a family. They had to take turns. Although Ann had overcome her fear of greenery, they realised she would not co-operate on these walks.

After her seventh birthday they decided to have another holiday. They chose Blackpool again—a holiday camp this time. There was no trolley to cope with, but the coach to the seaside produced the same screaming attack, until she was put in a seat with "dolly."

On their first day at the beach they hardly dared breathe as Ann looked at the sand for a few minutes and then rushed onto it picking up handfuls and throwing them in the air with squeals of delight. It was as though she was welcoming an old friend. Then she found a pool of sea-water left behind by the tide. First she put her toe in, then walked into it and then, joy of joy, lay down in it . . . laughing.

Jack sat in his deck-chair and pondered on the problem for hours. Surely if she could remember the things that had delighted her so long before, it was possible that there was something equally horrific locked away in that mind. If they could find it and destroy it surely, surely . . . ? She had found that water did her no harm when she fell in the puddle. Sand had become fun after she had been tipped from her trolley headlong into it. His mind turned the problem over and over again. There must be a key somewhere. If they could find it, then they could unlock the door to that troubled mind. But what was it? Was he clutching at straws? Was there no real significance in the water and sand?

If men and women so expert in the ways of backward children could not find the solution, what chance had he, an engineer? But he was her father. She was part of him. His flesh and blood. Why, you only had to look at her, golden-haired and blue-eyed and browned by the sun. She was perfect. There had to be a way. There HAD to be something.

By the time Jack had roused himself from his reverie the tide was almost at their feet and his unpredictable daughter hardened the thoughts that had been growing in his mind. She ran into the water and scooped up great handfuls, laughing with delight. That was not the action of a cabbage. She was reacting the way any normal child would in the sun-dappled sea.

The following day she also did something that any normal little girl can do. She got her brother into trouble. Leslie had spent a long time building his sand castle—complete with moat and water—and Ann jumped on top of it. In a rage the little boy picked up a bucket filled with wet sand and threw it at Ann. It missed. But it didn't miss the man sleeping a few feet away in a deck-chair. The sand caught him full in the face. That little bit of sisterliness cost Leslie a smacking.

Then on the last day something happened that they had dreaded for years. Ann lost "dolly." Wrapped up in the delight of sand and sea she had put it down for the first time in her life and when it was time to go home no one could find it. It was gone for ever, buried somewhere in that vast tract of golden sand. They waited with dread for the moment when the realisation hit Ann. But that moment never came. No screams, no tantrums. Nothing. It was as though "dolly" had never been. In a way the end of "dolly" was the end of an era, but even today there is not one member of the family who does not remember that ancient bottle and teat with affection. Everyone, except Ann, that is. She just laughs with delight when they tell her of her affection for "dolly."

They arrived home from that golden holiday more relaxed than they had ever been since Ann was born. The feeling that some kind of breakthrough was near filled their minds. They couldn't explain it, but the feeling was there. How or when it would come they hadn't a clue. They just knew they were tottering on the edge of something wonderful.

It came in the middle of the night. As Jack lay tossing and turning in his bed thoughts and dreams of Ann flickered through his half-sleeping mind. Then a voice whispered a word. Violence. The voice would not go away. It became louder in his mind, more insistent. Violence, violence, violence. "VIOLENCE," he shouted, and Ivy sat up fully awake.

Jack was sitting up too, his eyes glittering with excitement. The words tumbled over themselves in the rush to get out, but his mind was crystal clear. Violence was the answer, he told Ivy. It had been accidental violence that had ended Ann's fear of sand and water. Now if they were to use DELIBERATE violence—by smacking her every time she did something they did not want her to do—would it not have the same effect, and cure her of her fears? Ivy was horrified at the idea. They were not prone to smacking their children, and neither of them had ever raised a hand in anger to their daughter. Never.

Might it not have exactly the opposite effect and put her even deeper into her dark, little world, she asked. But Jack was determined and persuasive. He had had a vision, a dream, call it what you like, but he had seen so clearly in his mind's eye the answer to Ann's problems. He was sure he had found the key. Surely Ivy would not deny him the chance of unlocking the door? They had tried all sorts of conventional ways to get through to their child for the past seven years. None of them had worked. Surely they were not going to let this, perhaps the last, chance pass them by. Ivy was not over-convinced so they compromised. They would try it out over one particular issue. If it failed they would not try it again. They would forget it, and never even talk about it.

They agreed to try it on Ann's eating habits. Up to that point the only way they could feed her was to bring her in her little chair to the table, and force feed her from a spoon. She would not hold a spoon in her hand. When she had enough to eat she spat the rest out like a baby. Biscuits, bread and sweets had to be put between her lips, and when she required a drink that, too, was forced into her mouth.

Jack decided to start the very next day at dinnertime. Ivy spent a long time in the kitchen preparing the meal. She knew they had to go through with it, but she thought her heart would break.

First Jack took a straight-backed chair and placed it at the table. Then ignoring his daughter's screams he picked her up from her own little chair and sat her firmly in the dining chair. Ivy served the meal, took one look at her daughter and shut herself in the kitchen, a handkerchief between her teeth to stifle her sobs as she heard Jack smacking Ann to stop her struggling.

Their bewildered sons fled to Ivy after watching in horror as their father acted in a way they had never seen before. But the smacks worked. Ann's eyes opened wide and she stopped screaming. Jack picked up her spoon and forced it into her hand. She screamed again and threw the spoon down. He slapped her. Hard. He picked up the spoon again and put it in her hand. She threw it down again and got another slap.

Again the screaming stopped. Jack picked up the spoon again and forced it once more into her hand. Sweat was running down his forehead. He made her dip the spoon into the meal and forced it to her mouth. She spluttered and screamed, but she swallowed most of it. Every time she resisted he slapped her. Slowly the screams ended and he managed to force more food into her mouth from the spoon held in her own hand. Tears were blinding him. They mixed with the sweat that ran in rivers down his face, dripping off the end of his nose. He wiped them away with the back of his hand. He had started something and he was determined to finish it.

By the end of that meal Ann Hodges had fed herself for the first time. She was just over seven years old. Biscuits had been put in her hand and forced into her mouth. Every time she had tried to throw them away she was smacked. But the screaming had stopped.

Jack picked up his daughter and put her back in her little chair. Ivy and the boys were standing in the kitchen doorway. Ivy's eyes were bright with tears and the boys had eyes like saucers.

And then, as Ann sat rocking in her little chair,

tears—REAL tears—started to trickle slowly down her cheeks. Ivy couldn't stop herself, she ran over and hugged her beloved child. And although Ann struggled, it wasn't nearly as vehemently as before. Jack and Ivy held hands. They looked at each other, smiling through their tears and Jack kissed her. The boys, not really understanding but aware that something wonderful had happened, came over and hugged their parents. And they all stood looking at that sobbing little girl. It was the most wonderful moment of their lives. They were a complete family. Ann had joined them at last.

Now there was no time to be lost. Jack took a week off work and continued his heart-breaking system of getting Ann to feed herself. They brought in a refinement. Every time she did it correctly they gave her a cuddle. By the end of the third week the cuddles were more frequent than the smacks. They had won the battle. Ann was now feeding herself from the spoon, although she insisted on sniffing every spoonful before putting it in her mouth. In their ignorance Jack and Ivy Hodges had broken down the first barrier. They had found the key they had so long searched for. In fact, they had unwittingly stumbled on what is now considered an effective method of training autistic children—reward and punishment.

But on that day in 1959 they did not know this. They were desperate people who had resorted to desperate methods because of their love for their daughter. As they extended the method over the next few months they were too ashamed to tell anyone what they were doing. They were sure that outsiders would consider them cruel and heartless.

After their success with her eating habits they determined to take her disabilities one at a time and conquer them. They discussed her lack of personal cleanliness—she still used a pot, but only when forced to—but decided against that being the next step. Instead they would take her by the hand and force her to go all round the house with them.

She screamed terribly the first time they tried it, making her touch everyday objects for which she had shown fear. And those were more than could be numbered. At times the task seemed impossible. They would grip her firmly by the wrist and every time she resisted they smacked her. It had to be done. Gradually as the exhausting weeks dragged on her resistance was definitely becoming less. But each time they released her she would rush back to her little chair and sit rocking—and crying those wonderful real tears. They hugged her and loved her as often as they could and even that too she came to accept. Although she did not reciprocate, it was marvellous progress.

Then one wonderful night about two months later she got out of her chair and went to Leonard, took him by the hand and led HIM to the kitchen to the sink . . . and pointed to the tap. He poured her a glass of water. She took it and drank it. Jack and Ivy could not believe their eyes. They felt like dancing, or singing or doing something crazy. What a wonderful, cherished moment that was . . . even though Ann dropped the glass on the floor.

Jack was now sure that there was a considerable amount of intelligence in that little being waiting to be released. They encouraged the boys to take her by the hand and point things out to her. They took her out into the garden and all the time they talked to her. Those wonderful brothers, young as they were, entered into the spirit of things. They, too, realised that, with their help, they could at long last have the sister they had always wanted. The stranger that had so long bewildered them was going away.

Eventually she went out into the garden by herself. Only for a few minutes the first time but gradually she stayed there longer and longer. She pulled blades of grass, smelled them and threw them in the air. She plucked leaves from the trees and felt them in her hands. And she showed no revulsion for the worms the boys dug up for their fishing. In fact, they both landed in trouble the day Ivy found Ann with a dozen of them, laughing with delight as they wriggled in her hand.

Now it was time to teach her personal cleanliness. This was going to be Ivy's task. She forced her upstairs at fixed times every day and sat her on the pot in the toilet. Ann fought and screamed like a demon, but Ivy who was completely won over to the method of teaching her gave her a good hard slap. And again within a few weeks Ann found that resistance was useless and started to use the pot by herself. So they decided they had gone far enough with that part of her training and let her use the pot for a long time to come.

She was now communicating when she wanted something. She would take her parents or Leonard or Leslie by the hand and lead them to it. She still had her obsessions. The rocking sessions lasted for hours some days. Then she got a passion for lollipop sticks and her brothers would spend all their spare time going round the streets during the summer evenings picking them up for her. Ann, for her part, would spend hours laying them out in long straight lines on the floor, then breaking them up and starting all over again.

Discussions about her behaviour became almost like a council of war, deciding what would be the next best thing to try and teach her. Ideas were discussed and rejected. Whatever they did, they did together. They were that kind of family. It was agreed, for example, that they should try and get her to respond to shouted commands. She had never once shown any recognition for anything said to her.

They determined that whenever they could they would look her in the face and gently tap her on the nose and shout her name. Visitors to the house were even encouraged to do it. It had been going on for weeks without any sign of progress when Leonard came home from school one day. Ann was sitting in her chair and he walked up to her, tapped her gently on the face and shouted her name. There was no sign of recognition. She appeared to look right through him—the way she did with everyone. But as he turned to walk away her eyes suddenly moved and he was sure she was following his movements. He tried it again and definitely this time her eyes WERE following him. He rushed out to tell Ivy who was in the garden. She came in and walked up to Ann, shouted her name and started walking about the room. The little girl's eyes followed her every movement.

Ivy sat down and wept with joy.

From that moment, whenever her name was called,

Ann would look up and turn in the direction of the speaker. They were so delighted with her progress that they felt for a time that there should be more reward than just a hug. The idea was quickly discarded when they realised that if they gave her sweets they would put her in the same category as a performing animal.

After six months of concentrated effort Jack and Ivy took stock of the situation and they felt they had every right to feel pleased by what had been accomplished. Ann could feed herself, keep herself clean and was communicating by leading them by the hand. She was responding to her name, and showing very little reluctance now to being hugged.

Her brothers had really entered into the spirit of it all. Perhaps to them it was a kind of game. Jack and Ivy encouraged them to think of it that way. But whatever it was, there was little doubt that the sister who had ignored them for so long was now making attempts in her fumbling way to be one of them.

She would watch as they played with their toy cars. Gradually they would get her to take one of the little metal motors in her hand and roll it up and down the floor, just as they were doing.

If she dropped one they would shout, over and over again, "Pick it up," and eventually she appeared to understand. But there were still frustrating, confusing times. Once when she dropped a cup and Ivy told her to "Pick it up" Ann walked out of the kitchen and brought back a toy car. Ivy's spontaneous action was to pick the child up and hug her—and ignore the struggling protests.

Now it was decided to try and get Ann to come to

them when they called her name. They started by
getting Jack to hold her on his knee. But the screams
quite drowned the commands and no amount of
smacking worked. So next they got the boys to hold
her and either Jack or Ivy would say: "Ann, come
here," and the boys would push her in their direction.
It proved a dismal failure. As soon as Ann was released
she would race to her chair and sit there rocking.
They tried it day after day, week after week, but
there was no response. Always she would go back
to the chair.

Then one evening Ivy took a toy car out of Ann's
hand and walked away with it. Ann immediately got
out of her chair and followed her mother, trying to
snatch the car from her. The following evening they
did the same thing. But this time Jack held Ann and
Ivy walked upstairs with the little car and put it on
the toilet floor.

When Jack let her go she leapt from her chair,
ran upstairs, went into the toilet and picked up the
car. It was the first time in her life that Ann had
entered that little room of her own free will. Ivy had
killed two birds with one stone. In her intense eagerness to regain possession of the toy Ann had completely forgotten her fear of going into the toilet on
her own.

Over the next few days they were to try the same
little ploy over and over again and finally, but slowly,
they got her to come to them when they called. After
that it was a simple matter to discard the car entirely and just call her name. Slowly she came to
them.

But for all their success they realised that they were

putting an appalling burden on the child and on themselves. Everything that a normal child learned in the process of growing up, Ann would have to be taught. Everything they thought natural and commonplace they would have to show her, lead her to it and try to make her understand. The weight of responsibility was tremendous. They still didn't know for sure that they were doing the right thing and as yet they were too afraid to tell anyone. It was still so frighteningly possible that everything they were doing was wrong and harmful to the child.

However, they persevered and day after gruelling day they would take her from her chair and drag her round the house pointing out objects and repeating their name over and over again.

At times they would kneel down in front of her, take her hand and put it on her nose and say "Nose." First Jack then Ivy then Leonard and Leslie. Each one in turn would take that reluctant hand and put it on her face and say "nose." They would even repeat the actions in their troubled sleep, it had become so automatic.

The response appeared to be nil. Ann would snatch her hand away whenever she could and put it behind her back. But the breakthrough when it came was, in a way, unremarkable.

One day Leslie went up to her and said almost in parrot-fashion: "Where is your nose, Ann?" Just as he was about to take her hand and put it to her face, the little girl did it herself.

Their delight knew no bounds. They loved her and hugged her. Now they started on teaching her to point to her eyes, her mouth and her ears. And somehow it all proved so simple. She responded within a week and would answer the command immediately.

They progressed from there to objects in the house until she knew the sink in the kitchen so well that she became obsessed with drinking water!

Then one day Leonard asked Jack if he could have a dog. He loved animals and would spend hours looking enviously at the other pets in their neighbourhood. Jack had told him that they would consider buying a dog, but since then he had put off the idea every time it was raised. They knew that Ann had come a long way. She had conquered many of her fears, but they were minor compared to the terror she appeared to have for dogs.

If they brought a dog into the house the consequences could prove disastrous. Or it could achieve an undreamed of leap forward in Ann's struggle for normality.

They decided to give it a try.

Laddie

The Dogs' Home was only a few miles away and on a sunny Saturday morning Jack took Leonard and Leslie with him to choose their pet. That home was the local dustbin for all the waifs and strays that any city throws up. There were large dogs, small dogs and half-dogs. There were dogs with obvious pedigrees and there were mongrel dogs. There were sad dogs and happy dogs. There were dogs by the dozen.

The boys spent hours walking up and down between the rows of kennels. First they chose that dog because he looked so sad and lonely. Then they wanted this dog because he looked so frisky and full of fun. In truth they wanted every dog they saw. It was all becoming rather impossible so Jack took the phlegmatic, pipe-smoking man who was in charge of the kennels to one side. Did he have, he asked, a dog that was gentle, child-loving and house-trained? The man thought for a bit, looked at Jack and the boys and then pointed with his pipe. This way, he said.

They followed him away from the main rows of compounds to a kennel that stood back from the rest . . . and there he was. Large, brown—and dejected. He was leaning against the wire as though he had all the cares in the world. He looked so utterly dejected and lost. He was a cross between an Irish Wolf-

hound and God knows what else. He had a blind
eye and he was ugly. But on first sight they knew he
had to be theirs.

He cost five shillings, and that included a second-
hand collar and lead which seemed fitting for such a
second-hand dog. The man reckoned he was about
two years old, but you never could tell with one as
crossbred as that, he told them.

They walked him home, the boys taking carefully
worked out turns at who should hold the lead. Leonard could have him to the third lamp-post and then
it was Leslie's turn, and so on. He trotted beside them
as though he had been with them all his life. His head
was held high and his tail wagged as though it would
drop off. But their initial excitement was beginning
to wear off as they neared home. What would Ann
do? Jack had prepared the boys as best he could for
the ultimate disappointment. If she rejected the dog
completely then he would have to go back to the
home.

The fateful moment was put off, in fact, because
Ann was upstairs. The dog made himself immediately at home. He drank a pint of milk and polished
off the dinners which the boys were too excited to
eat . . . and curled himself up on the hearth rug.
Then Ann came into the room.

They waited for the screams, but no screams came.
She just covered her eyes with her hands and fled
back upstairs and wedged herself behind her cot.
Jack and the boys took the dog for a walk round the
neighbourhood and gave her time to come round.

When they got back she was sitting in her little
chair playing with shells they had collected on that

holiday of so long ago. As soon as she saw the dog she again covered her eyes and made for the stairs. But this time Jack held her. The dog stood looking at them, wagging his tail. Gently Ivy took the little girl's hands away from her eyes. They were tight shut. The boys brought the dog towards them and gently, ever so gently, Ivy forced Ann's hand in a stroking motion along his back. She continued to run her hand over that rough, matted hair and that wonderful creature put his head up and licked her face. Ann opened her eyes and looked at him. Then she pulled his ears and then she pulled his tail. She felt his legs and laughed with pleasure when he licked her hands.

And so started a beautiful companionship that was to last for twelve years. A miracle had happened. Ann's acute fear of dogs had vanished for ever. They called him Laddie and he turned out to be the most gentle creature one could imagine. She pulled him all over the house and not once did he resent it. He followed her everywhere and even stood guard when she was at the toilet. The boys loved him dearly and when he was not with Ann he would scramble and ramble with them through the woods. He became an honoured member of the little family.

When he died in January, 1971, there were tears of course. But he died at the end of a long life and a job well done. He had cured a little girl of a fear that had pervaded the dark corners of her mind for years and he brought joy to a family. No one would ever forget him.

The coming of Laddie seemed to herald a new upsurge in Ann's learning. She appeared to be more eager to go round the house with them in the endless task of having objects pointed out to her. Always Laddie was by her side and he in his strange way seemed to give her a new confidence.

It was slow, painstaking work. They would go for weeks without anything happening. Then she would lead them to something she wanted . . . always something new. And so it went on. But there would be days when Ann became withdrawn and would sit rocking in that little chair, crying softly to herself. It was as though she had withdrawn into that darkened little room in her mind where no one could follow. At moments like that they would leave her alone and let her cry for as long as she felt the need.

On one wonderful day Ivy could no longer bear the sight of that little weeping figure. She forgot all they had agreed and knelt down on the floor and put her arms round her daughter. Slowly Ann lifted her arms and put them round Ivy's neck and wept on her shoulder. They were all reduced to tears at that moment, but oh, how sweet they tasted.

They now began to notice that after these bouts of deep depression Ann would surge forward in her bid for knowledge.

It was after one of these two-day sessions of weeping that they discovered she had an ear for music. They had bought Leonard a transistor radio for his birthday. He carried it everywhere with him, and even took it to bed. But one morning he forgot to take it to school and Ann picked it up. She held it in her hands and then quite by accident she switched it on. First she held it to one ear and then the other.

When Ivy took it away from her she cried, and Ivy handed it back.

Again Ann held it to her ear and sat in her chair. She didn't even rock as she heard the music flowing all around her. She smiled. A real smile of joy. When the music stopped she started to cry and even started to scream. But Ivy wasn't having any of that. She smacked her and made her listen to the radio again until there was more music.

After that she was encouraged to listen to the larger radio in the house. They put her chair close to the speaker and she spent hour upon hour listening to it. To their amazement she cried when it was some deeply moving passage of the classics, and she giggled with delight when it was pop.

Convinced that she could differentiate between sounds they bought her a mouth-organ and after weeks of patience the boys taught her to blow and suck. She was absolutely delighted with the different sounds she could make. But this time they were determined that it would not become just another of her obsessions. The boys were encouraged to take it from her whenever they felt like playing it. So in this way Ann learned, for the first time in her life, that certain objects had to be shared.

Jack and Ivy felt they were killing two birds with one stone. They had taught her that everything they gave her was not her own private possession and they were sure the blowing and sucking motion would help her if she ever tried to speak. The mouth-organ also proved to be a welcome break from the monotonous lollipop sticks and the sea-shells as play things.

They were not setting themselves up to be experts on backward children, but they had every reason to believe they were becoming experts on Ann.

Of course they tried not to delude themselves. There were many days when they were subjected to the screaming fits. When she would rock back and forward in her chair. She would still bang her head against the wall if they were not watching and tear her hair out in handfuls. And she would try to rip her clothes off.

Those days they would wonder just how far they had progressed. They would be plunged back into the self-doubt of whether or not they were doing the right thing. But as Ann's moods passed so would the doubts be replaced with the hard facts that they had at least accomplished something.

Soon after this Ivy decided to take Ann to the local shops for the first time. Ann had at last begun to accept the new clothes that had been bought for her and had been taught to wear them without protest, once again by the method of slapping her into submission. No matter how much it hurt their hearts to do it, they had to admit it worked.

On that Thursday morning the little girl looked a picture as she trotted beside her mother. To all intents and purposes an attractive little girl out to help her Mummy with the shopping. Of course there was no conversation, and although proud Ivy tried to point things out to Ann she got no response.

But the idyllic situation lasted only until they got into the first shop—the grocer's. Ann immediately spotted the display of biscuits, rushed to it and picked up handfuls of biscuits. She sniffed them and then threw them in the air. Pandemonium. Ivy was horrified and so was the grocer. He thought the child had gone mad, but after Ivy stumbled through an explanation the man refused to take payment for the ruined biscuits.

Ivy for her part was determined that there would not be a repeat performance, and she was determined to make an example of Ann there and then. She took her by the hand and led her to the biscuit display. She shook her and slapped her legs and told her she was a naughty girl.

When she was satisfied that Ann had understood as well as she could, Ivy once again apologised to the grocer and gathering up the remains of her shattered dignity she marched Ann from the shop. There were no further incidents that day. But the following week in the same grocer's shop Ann made a bee-line for the eggs and, before anyone could stop her, smashed two of them on the floor. This time Ivy gave her a good hard smack and they never had any more trouble.

It was shortly after the egg-smashing incident that Ann went into a deep fit of depression. No matter what they did to encourage her she did not respond. She would sit in her chair from morning to evening just weeping and moaning . . . and rocking. At other times she would be absolutely still for hours. Just staring. Staring at nothing in particular. As those weary days grew into weeks their fears began to mount. They were now convinced that all was lost. Everything they had achieved had gone. The slappings, the tears and the heartbreak had all been for nothing. Ann had gone back to being a cabbage. They had lost her, perhaps for ever.

And then just as suddenly as it had arrived, the mood disappeared. Ann came downstairs one morning, ignored her chair and started walking around the house by herself, picking up all those objects they had so painstakingly shown her in the weeks before. She examined each object almost like a connoisseur trying to fix a value. Then she would slowly and carefully replace it and move on to the next thing that had caught her eye. In fact, this method of examining things became another of her obsessions over the next few weeks. But it was an obsession they encouraged. They were convinced that she must be absorbing and learning something from the objects.

Now they had another council of war. What next? It was decided they should try and stop Ann from that monotonous rocking. It was completely pointless. So all four of them Jack, Ivy and the boys whenever they saw her doing it would shout at her and slap her legs and tell her "naughty." The boys encouraged her to look at their comics and picture-books, although it is doubtful if much of it registered with Ann. But gradually, ever so gradually, the rocking became less and less as she became fascinated by the objects they showered on her.

One day Jack came home with a large bead counting frame and a set of wooden blocks with letters of the alphabet painted on them. And from that evening began one of the longest, hardest battles they were to face in the struggle to educate Ann.

As soon as Ann was given the blocks she set them out in a straight line. But Jack immediately broke up the line and re-arranged the blocks into squares. Ann was furious and put them back into a straight line. Again Jack broke up the line and arranged the blocks into a rectangle this time. Every spare minute was devoted to this silent battle of wills. When Jack was at work Ivy would take over the mind-boggling task. Every time Ann made the blocks into that straight line they would re-arrange them into a pattern. If Ann lost her temper and screamed they slapped her until she was quiet. But they did not slap her for making the straight line.

Then they switched tactics. They ignored the bricks and got her to concentrate on the bead frame. They would place it on the floor in front of her and put her hand on the coloured baubles and say "bead" over and over again day after day, week after daunting week, until the marvellous moment when they said: "Where are the beads, Ann?" and she immediately put her hand on the frame.

Next they took her fingers and placed them on the first bead and moved it from left to right saying "One," then "two," "three" and so on. Night after night they did it until, as with her nose and her name, they were saying it in their sleep. They were appallingly tired, and weary with concentration. But they plodded on, never losing their temper with her, never scolding her unless she started to scream. The mental effort was tremendous. They had become such a close family through their fight to teach Ann. They were united as one. When Jack or Ivy had to give up through sheer exhaustion the boys would take over. Night after night radio and television were forgotten in the single-minded task of counting those beads.

Then one night as they had a break for supper Ann was by the bead frame by herself. Up till then she had ignored it unless one of them was holding her fingers to the beads. Now she put her own hand to the first bead and moved it from left to right, blowing down her nose as she did so. Then the next bead and so on to the end of the frame. She kept blowing down her nose and just as Ivy reached for a handkerchief it hit them both at the same time. ANN WAS COUNTING. There could be no doubt about it. Each snort represented a number. They tested her. As she reached the fourth bead, Jack held the other six back and the blowing stopped. When he took his hand away and Ann moved bead No. 5 to the right she blew down her nose. And so with No. 6 up to No. 10 and when there were no more beads, she stopped blowing.

What a wonderful feeling engulfed them at that moment. Jack and Ivy hugged each other with delight, while Ann, oblivious to the excitement she had caused, went on pushing the beads and blowing down her nose.

Much as they wanted to, they knew they must not force her now that she had made the breakthrough. Instinctively they realised that too much too soon could well prove a disaster. So the following night they put the bead frame away and went back to the bricks.

As they expected, Ann immediately started by putting the bricks into a long line, but this time when they shouted at her she scattered them over the floor and started to arrange them again. But with a difference. Each time she picked up one of the blocks she blew down her nose until she had ten in one line, then she started another line, until she had another ten. And so she went on until she had used up all the bricks and had four equal lines.

It was the final proof they needed. Ann's education has really started. She was at last using her reasoning. What she had so painstakingly learned with the beads she was applying to the bricks. In the only way she knew how she had formed them into patterns . . . and she had counted them.

They were now determined to push ahead with all possible speed. Ann was ready and willing to learn. Of that they were sure beyond all shadow of doubt. However, to make sure that neither she nor they became bored they switched from beads to bricks on alternate nights.

They started to teach her to pick out differing numbers of beads on the frame at their command. Surprisingly, it did not prove as difficult as they had expected and within a matter of weeks she could pick out any number they told her, on any of the rows. They jumbled the numbers up, but she never faltered. If they said "six" she would move six beads along the frame, carefully blowing down her nose once for each bead. They bought her bags of little round sweets and she would carefully lay them out on the arm of a chair until the bag was empty and she had counted all the contents. Then, and only then, would she start to eat them.

Jack and Ivy realised now that they had started something that no one was going to stop. Night after night Jack would get on the floor with Ann and the bricks. He started by arranging them in alphabetical order and tried to teach Ann the ABC by guiding her hand to each brick. He hammered away at the system, night after night, week after week, but although her proficiency in counting them astounded them, they were sure she did not understand the alphabet. It was a problem that didn't take too much solving eventually. The answer was beautifully simple. Jack bought a second set of alphabet bricks!

He split the two sets up, one on one side of the floor and the other opposite. He then took Ann's hand and made her pick up the letter "A" and guided her until she had placed it on top of the "A" from the other set. He then repeated the performance with each block until the two sets were complete, each with the corresponding letter on top. Then he scattered them all over the floor and started again. And again. And again. It went on night after seemingly endless night. Mixing the bricks up, but always making sure that they ended up with the matched pairs.

As with so much they had accomplished the breakthrough came just when they were sure they could not stand any more. One evening when Jack scattered the bricks on the floor Ann simply picked up one and matched it to its neighbour, and so on until she had completed the whole sequence. The unfaltering way she did it left them astounded. It was as though she had been able to do it for years.

Now they went flat out in an attempt to identify each letter of the alphabet for her. They did it by holding the brick in front of her eyes and said the letter over and over before they let her put it on its neighbour. They encouraged the boys to speak to her in very simple sentences, identifying things as they did so. "Ann's coat," "Ann's Mummy," "Ann's Daddy," and so on day after day until she responded in the only way she could . . . by blowing down her nose. They bought simple jig-saw puzzles and spent hours making them up in front of her and then breaking them up again into pieces. Gradually they guided her hands and let her fit the pieces together until she was doing the whole thing herself.

The rocking was almost a thing of the past. She only reverted to it when she had nothing to occupy her. So every waking hour they took turns in trying to hold her interest. Their ideas didn't always work, of course, and there were days when she appeared to have switched off and gone back into that shell.

Soon it was time again for their half-yearly visit to the hospital doctor. It was a pouring wet day, but they knew Ann would not go on the bus. They decided on a taxi and although she raised a fair amount of objection, it was not nearly as bad as before and they kept up her interest all the way to the hospital by pointing out cars, shops and people on the pavo ment.

When they arrived at the hospital waiting room Ann immediately ran to the little chair she had sat in all those months before, and after carefully examining its legs, she sat down. The leg examination was something she had developed over the past few weeks. Before she sat on any chair she felt the legs. They were amazed that she had remembered the chair, and then just as she had done on the last visit she started to rock. But as soon as Ivy shouted to her she stopped.

When Ivy said: "Come here," Ann looked at her then slowly walked over to her mother—and climbed on her knee! It was the first time in her life that Ann had sat on anyone's knee of her own free will. By the time they had to go in and see the doctor Ivy had great difficulty in getting her eyes in focus because of the tears that just would not go away.

That wasn't to be their only surprise that day. As soon as the doctor opened the door she walked through to the little ante-room and straight into the sandpit. The doctor couldn't believe his eyes and said so. They told him of all the things they had tried to teach her and how she had responded. Jack was sure that as he spoke he was talking to a man who did not believe a word of it. When they had finished he looked at them for a few minutes and then asked them if he could test her with blocks and beads. They were delighted, but apprehensive. What Ann had done for members of the family she might not repeat for a comparative stranger. But their fears were groundless. She could not be faulted. She mixed up the bricks and the beads and counted them, as she did at home, by blowing down her nose.

The doctor was beaming by the time the little exercise was complete. He told them that the blowing was obviously a prelude to speech. It was the only way she could communicate because she just simply did not know how to use her tongue, teeth and throat to make sounds. He implored them to carry on and never to give up. He asked them how they had managed it and Jack and Ivy told him of the long nights of going over the same things again and again.

But they did NOT tell him that they started by slapping her. They knew it had worked. They knew it had been the key to finding their daughter, but somehow they were afraid of his reaction. They were unable to shake off that niggling feeling of doubt and guilt. So they kept their counsel.

Elated by the doctor's enthusiasm Jack asked him if he thought it was possible for Ann to be educated at a school. The answer was simple and direct. "Where?" There was nothing he would like better, but they had to face the facts. Her progress was little short of a miracle, but she could not communicate. Until she could talk there was no education authority in the country that would take her on.

"If she could speak even a few words, then there might be a chance," he told them.

With those words still very much in their minds they left the hospital. Their resolve was now greater than ever. If Ann had to speak before anyone would give her a place at school, then somehow they would find a way to teach her. They knew, as they had known for a long time, that in her present state she qualified for a place at an occupation centre for the mentally handicapped. But it was not education in the way they understood. It was just a place where those poor deranged children were kept happy and content. They were not taught to read and write.

They had come such a long way with Ann. They were not going to be beaten. Ann would be educated . . . at a school.

The First Word

Jack and Ivy Hodges hadn't the faintest idea of how they would set about teaching Ann to talk. But, they reasoned, everything she had learned so far had come from ideas born on the spur of the moment. They just knew she WOULD talk.

As they headed for home that day something happened that was to occupy their minds for several months, and from its small beginning bring forth the sound they so longed to hear.

It was raining heavily as they walked out of the hospital gates and they knew it would be foolish to attempt to walk home. Another taxi was out of the question. They simply couldn't afford the fare. Screams and all, they would have to bear. Like it or not, Ann was going home on the bus.

They hardly dared breathe as they waited in the shelter opposite the gates for the bus to arrive. They tried to keep Ann interested in things around her, but she didn't seem to respond. Then all too soon the moment they had dreaded arrived in the shape of the double-deck bus.

Ann got on without a murmur. She held Ivy's hand and allowed herself to be led to a seat. They felt they were dreaming. It just couldn't be possible. After all the years of screaming and hysterical outbursts, even when she saw a bus, their little girl had shown not the slightest fear.

They both pondered on the problem in silence for most of the journey while Ann sat staring straight ahead without a sound. Why? What had happened to make this change, this marvellous step forward? The answer came as they neared home. It lay in a conversational remark by Ivy. Had he noticed, she asked Jack, that it was a new-style bus? He hadn't really. His mind had been filled with wondering about Ann and her behaviour.

But it wasn't just a new bus, it was a different colour. It was green. All the other buses they had tried to get her to board had been red.

That was the answer. She was frightened of the colour red. There was no other explanation for her behaviour that day. The more they thought about it the more convinced they were that they had found the answer to another of her problems. Now they had to find out for sure. They thought back over other instances of inexplicable screaming fits and suddenly it struck them.

When they remembered those first few weeks at the new house they had become convinced that Ann was terrified of the trees and grass just because they WERE trees and grass. But now they were sure that the answer was more likely because of the colour, and they had cured her of that fear.

To test their theory over the next few days they bought her some cheap brightly-coloured poppet beads, including a number of red ones. They broke them up for her and gave them to the little girl. She started by laying them out in lines and counting them by blowing down her nose. But she would not pick up the red ones. The blues, greens, whites and even the pinks didn't cause any difficulties, but she would not touch the red ones. That was all the evidence they required. Another council of war, and it was decided that they should forget about ways of making her speak for the moment and concentrate on her colour problem. It was possible that if they could cure that phobia they might find the answer to so many others.

First of all they went round the shops and bought a large, violently red sponge. When Ivy used it on Ann she screamed and tried to get away from it in her bath. She was given a good smack and thoroughly washed with that sponge. Every time she needed her face or hands wiped they used the sponge. Within a few days she accepted it, and within a week she started playing with it at bath-times.

The next step was to buy her red socks and red slippers and make her wear them and slap her every time she tried to take them off.

Whenever they bought anything for the house where there was a choice of colour they chose red. So much so in fact that after two or three weeks they were all heartily sick of the colour. But after about six weeks they were congratulating themselves on having won another battle. Ann had grown to accept all the red objects around her, and even played with them in her obsessive way.

Their triumph was short-lived.

Convinced that they should give the experiment its final testing they took her out one Saturday morning and waited at the stop for a red bus. When it came Ann refused to get on, and screamed so much that no amount of smacking could stop her and they went home all terribly upset and utterly dejected.

What had gone wrong? They were so sure that they had got to the bottom of her problem with the buses and the colour, but that episode at the bus stop had proved just how wrong they were.

They thought long and hard about it. There was no doubt she had a fear of the colour red, but she had eventually accepted all those little red objects they bought her. THAT was it. Little. The bus was huge. Of course. It wasn't just red objects she feared. It was LARGE red objects.

But once they had reached that conclusion the problem was how to cure her of THAT fear. They couldn't face the idea of taking her to the bus day after day, week after week. They had to find some way of curing that fear in the security of their own home. That was easier said than done. They talked for days about what they could use and even seriously considered painting a wall bright red.

Then when she was out shopping one day Ivy saw a flag flying, and she remembered. They had a large Union Jack stored away at home. A relic from some half-forgotten celebration. She soon got it out. It was certainly large—it covered the entire living-room floor —and there was plenty of bright red.

That evening when Jack came home from work they waited until Ann was playing with the faithful Laddie in the kitchen and laid the flag out on the floor, entirely covering it. Ivy called Ann and she ran into the room and stopped on the edge of the flag. A look of horror was on her face. She just stood there staring at that huge splurge of red.

Gently they called to her to come to them on the other side of the room. After what felt like hours she did something that made them marvel at her intelligence, and laugh at the same time. Carefully, very carefully, she rose on to her toes and walked towards them, pointedly avoiding the red parts of the flag. Jack and Ivy walked to the other side of the room and called her again. Again she did the same thing, walking to them on her toes, avoiding the red. They called Laddie and he just strolled over the flag, flopped down and rolled on it. Then he sat up and watched Ann. Jack and Ivy moved to the opposite side from her and called her again.

By this time the horror on her face had been replaced with delight. She thought it was a game! She came over to them, again walking on her toes, and avoiding the red. So back and forth they all went. Jack and Ivy deliberately walking on the red, Ann avoiding it.

Then it happened. With all the strain of staying on her toes, one of her ankles gave way and she staggered on to St. George's Cross, slap-bang in the middle. She didn't make a sound. Gently they took her by the hand and walked her over that offending colour. They hugged her and loved her and then they put her to bed.

For the next two weeks they repeated the performance every night until she was walking on the red part without giving it a second glance.

Ivy then got a red blanket and put it on the floor, and without hesitation Ann walked all over it. They picked it up off the floor and put it round her shoulders. They let her feel how soft and warm it was. They encouraged her to cuddle it, and they put it on her bed. The very next day they took her once more to the bus stop. And when the red bus stopped Ann very slowly put out her hand and touched the paintwork. Then, and only then, did she take Ivy's hand and climb silently on board. This time there was no doubt about victory.

Never again was Ann to be frightened of any form of transport, whatever the colour.

That breakthrough did wonders for their morale and brought a great upsurge in their enthusiasm for their self-appointed task. It was as well it did. For shortly after that Ann went into one of her "moods" as they now called them. For the next two weeks she spent most of her time in her little chair softly moaning and weeping great tears. They could not console her, so they left her. But this time they did not feel despondent, although their hearts went out to that pathetic creature. Somehow they knew she would soon come round and be back with them.

During that long withdrawal period they discussed among themselves what they should do for her when she finally did come round. There was no doubt that she craved any form of learning, so they determined to see if they could teach her to identify colours.

When she did come back to them they put her through all the things they had so patiently taught her, and were delighted to see that she had not forgotten any of them. In fact, they were convinced she had actually improved. Now they were ready to teach her the different colours.

Ivy had got some ribbons—a red one, a green one, a white, a blue and a yellow and sewn them together in a circle. They put them on the floor and waited for Ann to pick them up. When she did she started to count them. Each time she put her hand on a different colour she blew down her nose. Then Jack and Ivy got down on the floor with her and each time she put her hand on a colour they shouted its name. Soon Ann took it to be some kind of game and when they were silent she would take their hand and put it on a colour before she blew down her nose. They persevered for weeks, shouting out the names. Those marvellous boys joined in and took over when their parents were almost too tired to speak. It was a long, hard and frustrating task. She kept getting them wrong. Then they realised that when they asked Ann to point to the red she would pick up the yellow. She never picked out the red. It was the old bugbear again. So Ivy removed the red ribbon from the circle and joined the others up.

They put the red ribbon on a chair. "Where is the red, Ann?" And she picked up the yellow. They took her by the hand and led her to the offending ribbon on the chair, and said "Red" to her. Then they said "Yellow" and walked her back to the ribbons on the floor and put her hand on the yellow one. They were back to the familiar pattern of repeating things night after night, but eventually she got the idea and started picking out the colours when asked. Ivy split them up and they placed the ribbons all over the room, and within a week she could identify her basic colours.

It was hard to believe that a whole year had gone by since they started on that course of trying to teach Ann. Was it really twelve months since Jack had picked up his daughter and slapped her into feeding herself? That moment of tears and triumph that would live with him all his days? It was time to take stock. She could feed herself, she had lost her fear of dogs, of buses and colours. She could count, in her fashion, and she could identify the letters of the alphabet. They had come a long way. They still had a long way—an extremely long way—to go. But when he looked at his daughter Jack knew it was all going to be worthwhile. Their achievements were tremendous, and he couldn't forget that it had all been born out of utter despair and hopelessness. The one thing that made it all so wonderful was to watch Ann with her mother. There was a growing affection from the little girl. At long last she was learning the meaning of giving love.

By now Ann responded almost immediately to their commands, but she would not look them straight in the eye. They tried holding her face with both hands and putting their own faces close to hers and talking to her. But she seemed to fix her eye on some middle distance and would not look into their eyes. They spent weeks telling her the names of objects, but her only response was to blow down her nose. Apart from that she did not make any attempt to speak.

There was no struggling sound fighting to get out, no attempt at anything but blowing down her nose. They told themselves that she wasn't ready and they switched back to the bricks and beads and colours, making up complicated patterns for her to sort out, and she did not fail them in this.

She was eight now and they desperately wanted her to have an education. If only those words would come they would get her into a school, or die in the attempt.

She now had started showing an interest in television, and with her brothers became a fan of children's programmes. She would laugh when they laughed, but Jack was sure she was only mimicking them. But strangely, somehow, she knew when it was time for her favourite programmes—even when the boys were not there. That was something they could not understand. It was uncanny in a way. They encouraged her to watch. Perhaps through television there would be the breakthrough.

It came on the evening of March 14, 1960. It is a moment that has lived with them all since. Jack, Ivy, Leonard and Leslie remember it today in all its simple clarity. There is no doubt that they will remember it for the rest of their lives.

Jack and Ivy were watching a quiz programme while the children played on the floor with their toy cars. A row blew up between the boys over one particular car. Jack angrily told them to be quiet, and they continued their argument in whispers. Leslie was trying to take a car out of Leonard's hand, saying "Yes" and Leonard was adamantly refusing to let it go, "No," he said. So it went on for a few minutes, those whispered words "Yes" and "No." And then suddenly there was another whispered voice.

Ann had a car in one hand and was pulling it with the other saying "YEH" and then pulling it back and saying "NAH." What a marvellous moment!

The television was switched off and Jack and Ivy were on the floor beside their children. Tears blinded them, but they encouraged the boys to keep whispering. Their argument was forgotten in their excitement. Young as they were, they realised that the moment so long dreamed of had come true. They pointed out objects to her and said their names, and that beautiful, wonderful sound came from the little girl. She whispered the names after them. It was true. It was actually happening. Ann was talking.

ANN COULD SPEAK.

Jack looked at Ivy and emotion swept over them like a wave. They hugged each other and wept. They hugged Ann and the boys. They stayed on the floor crying and laughing at the same time, getting her to say more and more things and she responded magnificently. But before she said each word she blew down her nose. The doctor had been so right. It had been a prelude to this magnificent evening.

In place of the walking vegetable they had so feared they now had a daughter who could think and talk. True, her words would not be easily understood by anyone outside the family for a long time to come. But that was nothing.

They all threw themselves into encouraging her speech. Within days she was whispering such things as "drink, water," "coat on," "My chair" and many others. They bought little picture books and spent countless hours going over the objects with her and getting her to say their names. They discovered that she only responded when the words were whispered to her. Anything said in a normal voice met with a blank stare.

Then as suddenly as it began, her talking stopped.

She refused to acknowledge them and spent days just walking about the house, looking at the objects that had for so long fascinated her, but she refused to utter a sound. They were sure it was a milder form of one of her "moods" and they left her very much on her own. The suspense was dreadful. They wanted so much to help her push ahead with her talking and learning, but she had left them for the moment and there was nothing they could do about it.

Then she came back to them, having once again forgotten nothing they had taught her. She was full of energy and quite tired them out. It was as though during these withdrawal spells she had become recharged.

They tried to encourage her to put more sound into her words, and in fact it was television that came to their aid. They noticed that she would start humming some catchy tune she heard on a programme, and she would hum quite loudly. It was amazing. She had the ability to retain a tune, even though she had only heard it once. At these moments they would raise their voices slightly from the now-accepted whisper and she would repeat the words in a slightly louder tone. And so it went on until she was quite audible to everyone.

Jack and Ivy were beside themselves with delight and decided to take the plunge. They applied for an interview with the local education authority. It was time Ann received some kind of formal education.

Eventually, after weeks of waiting, they were summoned to take Ann to the education authority doctor. They had spent the time encouraging her with her speech, helping her to identify objects from her little books and generally preparing her for the ordeal ahead. They knew the interview wouldn't be easy and they were filled with apprehension when the great day arrived.

Their fears were well-grounded.

The doctor was a busy man and didn't appear in the least interested in Jack and Ivy's story of Ann. He wanted to find out her capabilities for himself, he told them. First he gave her a full physical examination.

Then he produced a number of coloured picture cards and handed them to the little girl and told her to identify them. It was a hopeless failure. She only opened her mouth once and said one of the pictures was of a train. The doctor was peremptory. "It's an engine," he said. He turned to Jack and Ivy and told them that she had failed the test and there could be no question of her getting a place in one of the schools. The couple were on the verge of tears. Years of struggle and heartbreak were being washed away in a fifteen-minute interview by a man who didn't even want to hear them tell of the marvellous progress their child had made.

It was at that moment Jack broke the habit of a lifetime. He lost his temper. He told the doctor, implored him, to phone the child psychiatrist at the hospital. Reluctantly he agreed. After what felt like a lifetime he returned. Their hearts leapt up. His attitude had obviously changed. He was full of praise for what they had done. But their hopes were quickly dashed. His attitude may have changed, but not his opinion. He made it obvious that Ann was not ready for a place at one of the council's schools.

Although he told them that their application would be considered and he would send for them if it was successful, they left the office with a heavy heart. They knew that he would not recommend Ann for a place. They waited for three weeks, but still there was no news and Jack decided to take matters into his own hands. He had vowed that if Ann made the breakthrough with her speech he would have her educated. She had made the breakthrough and he was going to get her educated even if he had to go through the back door and cut the red tape away with a hatchet.

He had a friend on the council and told him of the interview. He invited the man to come to his home and see just what Ann could do. The councillor had known the family for a number of years, but had not seen Ann for about two years. He was astounded at the progress she had made and asked Jack for a photograph of her. He took it away with him and said he would be in touch. A week later they received a letter from the Director of Education saying that Ann was to be given a "trial" at a small school for the educationally subnormal.

They were not to learn for many years from their friend, just before he died in fact, that he had gone straight to the Medical Officer of Health with the picture of Ann. He threw it on his desk and asked him what he thought of her. The Medical Officer thought her a beautiful child, "Is she yours?" he asked. "No," said the councillor. "She is yours, and you are neglecting her."

Then he explained about Ann. For an hour they talked about the little girl and the fight her parents had put up to give her a life. Now the chance of an education would slip away if something wasn't done rapidly. They contacted the psychiatrist and the Director of Education who agreed that the child could have a trial at the school.

In his letter to Jack the Director of Education suggested that they should take Ann along to the school and meet the headmaster and have a full discussion with him.

They didn't waste any time. They made an appointment to see him the very next day.

That meeting turned out to be the beginning of a wonderful friendship that has lasted through the years. The headmaster knew quite a bit about Ann. The psychiatrist had explained as much as he could about her. But before he had even seen her he had decided to take her on at his little school. It was only years afterwards that he was to tell Jack and Ivy that the original trial period was for two weeks only. He was asked by the Medical Officer of Health to assess the child and report back. But when he saw the parents and the enthusiasm they had for their daughter's capabilities he kept them ignorant of that fact.

He told them on that first momentous meeting that he wanted to "set his stall out." Ann's education would have to be a combined operation. Jack and Ivy were only too willing to put themselves under his command and agreed to follow everything he suggested for her education. He was that kind of man. Remarkable. His name was George Glover.

Right Hand—Left Hand

I

It was really the war, or rather the carnage at the very end, that put George Glover on the road to teaching educationally sub-normal children.

Originally, he had intended studying physics, but the bomb at Hiroshima ended that dream. He suddenly realised that he wanted to help people less fortunate than himself. "After VJ Day," he said, "it was a desire to put something back into this big pot. We had taken so much out."

So when he was discharged with the rank of Major, he opted to go to teacher training college, where he specialised in the problems of backward children and the educationally sub-normal. He studied psychology, and eventually became an Associate Member of the British Psychological Society.

Teachers of his calibre were at a premium and he had no difficulty getting a post in Salford where he lived. Soon his remarkable ability to get through to educationally sub-normal children was being noticed and within a few years he was given a headmastership. Many of his methods were unorthodox and shocked the purists, but he got results. Something that was to become evident in his dealings with Ann.

The first time he saw her, it was obvious to him

that she was severely disturbed. But even then he could detect the difference between her condition and that of the maladjusted children he had been dealing with. On the whole they were always seeking attention, yet disobedient. They were extremely dull. One learned to detect that type of child by sight. Ann was something different. She had a strange look in her eyes. It was wild, not vacant.

While he was talking to Jack and Ivy he was noting all the time the things that she did. For example: she was taking a great deal of interest in his desk. She examined its legs, and underneath it. She played with a vase of flowers on top.

George Glover realised at that moment that to have refused to take the child into his school and deny her the chance her parents craved would have been the worst thing he could have done. He said many years later that it would also have been the worst mistake of his career.

As he looked at the child that day he was sure that he knew what was wrong with her, but he didn't voice an opinion. He wouldn't, until he was certain. But the way she acted and reacted to things was distinctive. He had seen it before in another child. Of that he was sure.

For the moment they must press ahead. He had only those two precious weeks. If they were going to succeed he needed everyone's co-operation. He told Jack and Ivy they must do as he suggested, and they were only too willing to agree. He took his staff aside and told them in his blunt, no-nonsense fashion that they must observe her every moment she was at the school. Observe and note.

But towards the end of the first week it had become clear that the magnificent work being done by the teachers wasn't enough. He needed more help. Unorthodox men do unorthodox things. What George Glover did was, he admitted many years later, way-out even for him.

After morning assembly he called all the children together and explained his problem . . . and asked them to help.

Quietly he told them all he could about Ann. They had all seen the way she behaved, how she would hit herself on the face with her hands, try to rip her clothes off and bang her head against the wall. She was having a bad time, he told them. If they didn't help him to help her she would not be able to stay at their little school. He told them how much he wanted her to stay with them so she could have the chance of being educated. The same chance as they were getting. He couldn't do it alone. Without their co-operation she would have to leave.

They listened to him in silence, hanging on every word. This man who was their helper and friend, who had given all of them at some time the hand they needed to cross the more difficult hurdles in their life.

Now he needed help. THEIR help. How could they refuse? What he wanted them to do was simple. Every time they saw her trying to take her clothes off they were to talk to her. Try to stop her. Gently. They were to go out of their way to be friendly. She wouldn't talk back to them, but they weren't to let that stop them. Just keep talking to her. Let her know they loved her and wanted her as part of their little school. Their family. If they stayed with her they could prevent her banging her head, they could help her downstairs when she appeared to have difficulty. They could help her on and off with her coat and hat. If all else failed they would always be on hand to call a teacher.

He had won them over. Their enthusiasm knew no bounds. From that moment on while she was at that school, Ann was never on her own. Always there would be some of those wonderful children to help her. A remarkable achievement when one remembers that each one of those children had their own problems. But, without exception, love flowed from them in an endless stream and engulfed that pathetic little girl who was at the same time one of them, and yet so different.

By the end of the second week George Glover was able to tell the Medical Officer of Health that in his opinion, Ann was educable and he wanted her at his school.

The children's enthusiasm for helping Ann never waned, and in fact it had to be curtailed. After about six weeks the headmaster found himself addressing them again. Ease up a bit, he told them. Their love was smothering her. She could do more than they would allow her to do. They must keep on helping her, but they shouldn't fuss over her so much. They just had to let her know she was one of them. That she belonged.

George Glover was now convinced that Ann was autistic. The way she acted was exactly like the little boy he knew . . . a close member of his family. He, too, was autistic. As far as behaviour patterns were concerned they could have been twins.

It was one of those strange quirks of fate that had brought this man and this little girl together. He had the previous knowledge and the ability to see that Ann was more than just maladjusted.

Otherwise he might easily have gone along with the description that she was a psychopath. Or even an epileptic. But in George Glover's experience there was a great difference between the epileptic child and the autistic. Although both could be violent, the epileptic applied his violence to the outside world, the autistic child mostly to himself.

Although he knew that Ann was autistic he didn't know how it had happened. No one did. He questioned Jack and Ivy closely, but they couldn't suggest anything that might have been the cause. In the case of the little boy in his family it was vastly different. They knew the exact moment when he became autistic.

He was two years old when he fell in a rain-swollen river. Fortunately he had been taught to swim from the first few months of his life, or he would have drowned. He was washed up against a plank that had been jammed against the river bank and banged his head. A huge bump told them that. But he managed to work his way along the plank and held onto some tree roots on the river bank. He hung there screaming. He screamed for two hours before anyone found him. When he was finally rescued, he was unable to speak or communicate in any way. He was completely withdrawn. He was autistic.

Although Ann was beginning to behave much better at school—the screaming fits were much less frequent—she wasn't showing any inclination to read or write, despite patient hours spent by the teachers, headmaster, Jack and Ivy.

This was a serious problem. There wasn't much chance of her making progress with any other form of schooling if she couldn't read. George Glover pondered on the problem hard and long. There had to be an answer somewhere. But what? He went over every scrap of information he had about the child, including medical reports. They didn't tell him anything he didn't already know. She was physically perfect. There didn't appear to be anything wrong with her hearing and her eyesight was good, according to the doctors. Her predominant eye was her left one, said the report.

George Glover sat up with a start. He re-read that part of the report. He was keenly aware of the importance of the theory of mixed lateral dominance. There was a pronounced deterioration in a child's ability to learn by visual means if the child suffered from it. The theory had first been given by an American neurologist. It had been independently researched by two leading British psychologists who came to the same conclusion as the American.

Simply, mixed lateral dominance meant somebody whose "leading" eye was the opposite to their "leading" hand—left-handed right-eyed, right-handed left-eyed. To find out the leading eye doctors used a rather simple method. They covered a child's eye with a card and then waved a pencil in front of the other. Then they repeated it the other way round. The eye which followed the pencil most accurately was the leading eye.

If the child was right-eyed, then he should be

right-handed and, of course, left-eyed meant left-handed.

In his readings on the subject George Glover had come across a much more sophisticated test which was meant mainly for adults, but he had adapted it for the children at his school. He normally gave each of them the test when they came to the school, but so far Ann hadn't been put through it.

The test consisted of a card with a hole punched in the middle. When it was applied to adults they looked through the hole from a distance of about fourteen inches at a certain object. When they closed the dominant eye the object vanished.

In the headmaster's version, he put a toy on the table and got the child to look at it through the hole in the card. When he was sure they had their eyes firmly fixed on the toy, he would remove it and replace it with his eye. Rather like sighting a rifle. He could look down the "sight" and straight into the dominant eye.

He decided to try it out on Ann. But it was a lot easier said than done. She couldn't understand what he wanted her to do. He told her it was a game. They called it bo-peep. He brought in one of the teachers to hold the card. But over the next few days it took hours of painstaking work and subterfuge to get her to look at the object. Then he removed it—and looked along his "sight." Ann was right-eyed. He couldn't believe it. Surely not. But he tried it again and again. Laboriously they carried out that experiment six times.

Now there was no doubt. She WAS right-eyed. Predominantly so, in fact. This now meant that they would have to concentrate all their energies on getting her to use her right hand. By this time she was almost ambidextrous, some days using her left hand, some days her right. Surely this was what was causing her confusion over reading and writing.

But before he took that step he asked the medical officer to re-examine her and tell him which was her dominant eye. Using the pencil method the doctor came up with the same answer as the headmaster. The right eye.

Next he told Jack and Ivy to make sure that she used her right hand in everything she did and explained to them what he had discovered. Everyone at the school now threw all their energies into getting her to write with her right hand. It was no easy task. She kept wanting to change hands, but they persevered and within six weeks she was using her right hand exclusively.

From that moment there was a great surge forward in her learning and soon she was reading and writing simple sentences.

Much to George Glover's delight there was a side-effect bonus. Ann was attending a speech therapist once a week, and after they got her using her right hand, the speech therapist wrote to the headmaster to say that there had been a remarkable improvement in Ann's speech.

There was no doubt that it was due to making her use her right hand. Most educationalists knew that in the "bad old days" when children who were naturally left-handed were made to use their right it often affected their speech. With Ann, they had done the reverse. It was the turning-point.

George Glover had realised that being unable to read was the most emotionally-loaded inability in a child's school-life. They could get by without being able to understand arithmetic. For sport-minded boys the inability to play football or excel at games might worry them, but nothing like being unable to read.

And, of course, it had its emotional moments for the teachers, too. There was a feeling of indescribable elation when they saw a child suddenly break forth and read after weeks, sometimes years, of not having understood a word. Those were the moments that made a life-time of dedication so worthwhile.

The effect on Ann was nothing short of amazing. This ability to read gave her a new confidence. She became more affable with the other children and she started behaving much more naturally.

They had made the breakthrough just in time, as it turned out. For shortly after this the headmaster was told that Ann must have a reading test to find out if she could continue at his school, or whether she should be switched to a centre for the uneducable— something her parents dreaded.

If she could read, she was educable. If she couldn't, she wasn't, was the basic yardstick.

On the day the inspector arrived, Ann was taken into the headmaster's study for the test, which proved to be a stringent one. Fortunately she was no stranger to that room. She had spent many hours there going over her reading. She read, and she passed with flying colours. Now there was no question of her being transferred, something that had been hanging over her head from the day she entered the school.

And so she remained with George Glover at that

school until she was twelve. She should have left when she was eleven, but he put in such a strong plea for her that the education authority relented.

He wasn't implying, he told them, that his school was any better than any other, but Ann had shown such a surge in learning between her tenth and eleventh birthdays that it would be a pity to interrupt her at that point. If they allowed her another year with him she would have more than likely consolidated that gain.

Just before she left his school after her twelfth birthday, George Glover tested her reading ability. She registered a reading age of seven-plus. "I was rather pleased," he said simply many years later, "especially when you remember that many adults never get much beyond a reading age of nine."

When she left that little school it was, in a way, the end of her beginning.

II

The day Ann started at George Glover's school brought many practical problems for Jack and Ivy. Not the least was getting her there. The education authority were sympathetic, but transport was out of the question, they said. So every day Ivy escorted her daughter the four miles there and back. It put a tremendous strain on her. She would have to get up at 6:30 a.m. to get Jack ready for work. Then she would make breakfast for Ann, the boys and herself, and get the boys ready for school before setting off with Ann.

They had to take two buses there and then Ivy

would get two buses back home in time to prepare a
meal for Jack and the boys. Then it was time to go
for Ann again. She carried out that routine every day
for four years. It was only a long time afterwards that
she admitted that towards the end of each week she
was nearly out on her feet. But Ivy was a fighter. She
had fought long and hard alongside her husband to
get a better deal for their daughter. She wasn't going
to let a little thing like travel put her off.

As they watched Ann progress over the next few
weeks they could only marvel at the improvement she
was making and at the way the other children were
helping their daughter. Those children even taught
Ann to use the toilet, something that had defeated
them at home. So another bridge had been crossed.

Ann was now becoming obsessed with speech. She
tried so hard sometimes that she would fly into a rage
when she was unable to make herself understood,
and they had to resort to the old method of smacking
her to bring her round. They spent many sleepless
nights because of her constant chatter, but they didn't
want to discourage her. She echoed everything that
was said to her. If a neighbour said: "Hello, Ann," she
would say "Hello, Ann." She still had difficulty making
full sentences and would just say the basic words. It
was suggested she should have speech therapy lessons and she began to improve. Then came the marvellous breakthrough with her reading and writing
and she surged forward.

But there were still those periods of tantrums.
Fastening buttons was a major task and when the
other children tried to get her to play with a ball she

found it impossible to catch it. She would cry with frustration and their hearts would go out to her.

Then she fell out with the radio that had so long been her companion. She refused to listen to it. If it was switched on when she came into the room she would switch it off. They never did find out why.

She also had a strange obsession about television. She refused point-blank to watch any BBC programme. No matter what it was they had to switch to the commercial channel. If they refused she just sat and cried.

She was now growing rapidly and they realised that they would have to do something about her sleeping arrangements. The boys slept in single beds in their room. There was the little room waiting for Ann, but she refused to go into it. It was the room in fact where she had spent that terrible first day when they arrived at the house all those years ago. They hoped one day she would take to it, and make it hers. As it was she still slept in her cot in their bedroom.

The cot was old and battered, and falling to bits. So one day while she was at school they went out and bought a single bed and put it in place of the cot . . . still in their bedroom.

Ann was horrified and would not have anything to do with it. They took her into the boys' bedroom and showed her their beds. They encouraged her to jump on them and bounce up and down, and soon she was giggling with delight. Then they took her back to the new bed and let her jump on that, and finally she accepted it. But she insisted on sleeping with her feet at the head of the bed, with her body pressed close to the wall. She was to sleep in that fashion for years. But they didn't worry. They had solved the problem of the cot.

She was discarding some obsessions, and at the same time gathering new ones. They had been encouraging her for months to play with the jig-saw puzzles, until suddenly that too became an obsession. Every spare minute she would play with them, until she could almost do them with her eyes closed.

Then she became afraid to sit down anywhere except at her desk at school and on the stairs at home. She even insisted on standing at mealtimes. They let her carry on in this fashion for a week or so, quite sure that it would pass. But it didn't and Jack once again had to become firm with her. She had to be slapped into submission, but she was soon sitting down when she was told.

But there were moments of high good humour with some of these strange obsessions. She became fascinated by hands, anyone's hands. Even complete strangers'. She would go up to them in the street and put her hands in theirs and just murmur with pleasure. Jack and Ivy spent many embarrassing moments explaining about Ann to the equally embarrassed people.

It was even worse when she switched her affection from hands to legs. It caused great hilarity in the house when she would go to the male visitors and roll up their trousers, and start stroking their legs. It was brought to a halt with a good smacking after she tried it on the bus with the conductor! Ivy decided it had gone far enough.

They now began to wonder if they could encourage her to play with toys. She had never shown the slightest interest in dolls, but they thought it was now worth a try. Full of hope they went out and bought four small rag ones and gave them to her. She held them in her hands and insisted on taking them to bed with her.

At last their little girl was acting like any other little girl, playing with dolls. It was a wonderful feeling.

When they went up to bed that night Ann was still awake. The dolls' bodies were lying discarded on the floor and she was playing with the heads, lining them up along the bed. They felt sick with horror. Why she had done it was beyond their comprehension.

They decided not to repeat the experiment and instead they bought her a garden swing. It proved a huge success and she spent many hours playing happily on it. It seemed to soothe and relax her until, like many other things, it became an obsession. She could hardly wait to get home from school and get onto it. She would shout with pleasure as she went zooming back and forward.

But there were times when she would sit quite still on it and just gaze around her. At those moments Leonard and Leslie would go out to her and point out the various flowers and get her to repeat the names. It touched Jack and Ivy deeply to watch their children together, the boys enthusiastically encouraging her to say the names after them and telling her she was a good girl when she got it right. Then she would laugh with pleasure.

By the time Ann was ten the tantrums were fast

disappearing and when they did rear up they didn't have to do so much slapping. They found that by talking to her sternly they could shake her out of her moods. Life was certainly looking good.

One day she arrived home from school with a skipping rope. It was a present from George Glover. He had seen the wistful look in her eyes as she watched the other little girls playing the skipping games that had been handed down from generation to generation. She had so desperately wanted to try it for herself, so he got her the rope.

She insisted on trying it out on the garden path that evening and for hour after hour she tried to master the art, but it was hopeless. She just couldn't do it. They brought her into the house weeping bitter tears of tiredness and frustration. Every evening that week she took the rope out to the path and attempted to copy the girls she had seen at school, but she failed miserably.

Her hands and feet just would not co-ordinate. She tripped herself up. She fell. She tried for hour after hour, but could not skip. They tried to help her, but it was no use. Then Leonard came up with the solution. He tied one end of the rope to a drain pipe and turned the other end for her. After a few attempts she got it right. She could skip. The joy on her face was a sight to behold. She laughed with delight—and she was tireless, a fact which created its own problems. Eventually Leonard became tired, and Leslie took over. Then it was Ivy's turn, then Jack. They were all exhausted by the end of that evening. All except Ann. Now she expected them to be out every evening with her turning the rope. But within three weeks she had another attempt with the rope on her own—and this time she got it right.

For the first time in her life she was playing an ordinary child's game. Up until then she had been inclined to stay on her own and kept to herself during play-time at the school. Now she could take part in skipping games with the other girls. True, she was ungainly in her movements, but at least she was joining in. It did wonders for her morale. She seemed more cheerful and brighter.

During a routine visit to the family doctor, he suggested that Ann should have her tonsils out. He was convinced that it might help her with her speech. They carefully prepared her for her two-day stay in the hospital, explaining as best they could about the operation, but she didn't appear to be worried. However, they had to promise to buy her something special for coming home. A blue, whistling kettle!

A few weeks before she had developed the most peculiar obsession of her young life—for coloured kettles. Her teacher bought her a silver one, a green one and red one. She didn't really do anything with them, except hold them in her hands and gaze at them with rapture. There wasn't another house in Salford that had so many kettles.

The operation passed without incident. They took her in one morning and brought her home the next. She looked a little pale, but none the worse, and when she got home, joy of joys, there it was. Her shiny blue, whistling kettle. Ann still has that little kettle today. They kept it for sentimental reasons and she laughs with delight when they remind her of that strange obsession.

The tonsils operation proved to be a huge success because from that day she could pronounce her words much more clearly and there is no doubt the operation made a tremendous contribution to her ability to speak properly.

Shortly after Ann had been in hospital, her teacher began sending her home with small exercise books containing her attempts at copying from the blackboard and a request that Ivy and Jack should encourage her to draw at home.

Most of the drawings were of humans, with very long legs, arms and feet and tiny bodies. The eyes were where the mouth should be, and vice-versa.

They bought her a slate and pencils and taught her how to rub out and start again, and they encouraged her to copy from some of her picture books. The headmaster warned them not to force her. So when she lost interest they let her do as she pleased until she felt like drawing again. It was the same method as used in school.

They were now delighted by the amazing clarity of her voice and she made them laugh many times by expertly mimicking her teacher's commands. She was also trying extremely hard to copy the alphabet, but for the moment all her writing was either back to front or upside down, but the teacher told them not to worry. It was something she would eventually get over, she said.

The teacher also started her on needlework and the first little mat she brought home is still among Ivy's proudest possessions.

Ann was now questioning them about everything.

Day and night she would ask about this and that and they had to find ways of telling her in the simplest fashion, so that she would understand.

Soon she was eleven, and it was time for her to be considered for the senior educationally sub-normal school. George Glover sent word to Jack that he would like to have a discussion with him. The headmaster told Jack that he was going to apply for a year's extension. He was delighted with her progress, he said.

She was taking part in most of the school activities and even joined in the singing at music lessons. She could repeat all her tables up to six by heart. Whether she really understood them was a different matter, but it certainly proved to everyone that she had a fantastic memory.

Those two men were united in a single aim. Ann's education. They spent three hours that day discussing every aspect of the little girl, her past, her present and her future. Jack knew in his heart that if she could stay even for another year at that school it could bring about the answer to so many more of her problems. A few days later George Glover got in touch with him to say that the extension had been granted and he would be moving Ann to a higher class.

She soon settled down with her new teacher and her desire for knowledge grew every day. There were still upsetting set-backs. For example: she developed a fear of fruit skins and couldn't bear to touch them. Then she wouldn't look at any kind of meat. She would run away from the table at mealtimes if there was meat. After heartbreaking days of forcing her back to the table they managed to get her to join in, but they could not get her to eat meat of any kind.

So once again Ivy had to resort to subterfuge and made up dishes with the meat disguised among potatoes. They got her to drink fruit juice, because she would not touch fresh fruit and in this way they made sure she got an adequate supply of vitamins.

Physically she was perfect. She was tall for her age, and she had that beautiful peaches and cream complexion, and big, blue, tragic eyes. Everyone fell in love with those eyes. They were so sad. It was as though they had taken in all the sorrows of the world and could not let them go.

At school the women in charge of meals mothered her and looked after her during the breaks. For as yet she had not learned any sense of danger and they were always on hand if games became too rough or got out of hand. They even joined in her skipping rope sessions and played ball with her, although she only caught it by good luck rather than judgement.

So the weeks passed into months, marked by minor triumphs and frustrating set-backs. She was now deluging them with questions. Some so constructive as to be remarkable, others so garbled that they could not understand them. They had to answer all she asked. She demanded it of them.

Then she went into one of her withdrawal periods. She did not talk to them for days and just sat in her little chair, rocking. Once again they left her. But it was to be for the last time. When she came back to them, full of chatter, her search for learning took a leap forward and the rocking was gone for ever. Only

once more in her life would she sit in that chair and
rock. But that would not be for a few years—and for a
very different reason.

Now she was washing and dressing herself; she
could tell her full name and where she lived to anyone who asked; fastening buttons was no longer a
problem. She used a knife and fork with practised
ease and she could fasten her shoes.

One day they visited some friends at a new house.
They were shown round and Ann was with them. The
couple pointed out the room that was to be their
daughter's bedroom. Ann listened in silence. But when
they got home she took Ivy by the hand and led her
upstairs to the little bedroom. "My bedroom," she
said.

The next day Jack and Ivy went out and bought
furniture and then moved the bed from their room
into the little bedroom. Ann agreed to sleep in it that
night, provided the curtains were left drawn back
and the door open. They were only too happy to
agree. That night for the first time in her life Ann
Hodges slept on her own. She was almost twelve years
old.

When they went up later in the evening to peep
at her they found their way barred—by Laddie who
had stretched himself out on the mat outside her door.
It was as though he too knew she was on her own
for the first time.

That week they decided to try her once again
with some dolls. Even if she didn't play with them,
they would always decorate her bedroom. She didn't
pull their heads off this time. Instead she found a
pair of scissors and cut their hair off. Then she took

all their clothes off and bound their legs, bodies and arms with bandages.

It suddenly dawned on Ivy that what Ann wanted was boy dolls. The following day she made some little trousers and jackets for the dolls and Ann played for hours taking off and putting on their clothes, but only when she wasn't concentrating on her reading, which was progressing by leaps and bounds. They were delighted, although not frankly surprised, when told that she had passed for the senior educationally sub-normal school.

But that episode of her life was to prove a dismal failure.

Rejected

The weeks between Ann leaving the junior school and her move to the senior educationally sub-normal school were nerve-racking for Jack and Ivy. They realised only too well it could prove to be a huge step forward in her quest for knowledge and her fight for normality, but they couldn't help wondering if the step would prove too much for her. She had come so far in such a short time. However, they convinced themselves that it was for the best and they spent as much time as they could encouraging her to continue her reading and writing. She didn't really need much prompting. Her desire to learn now knew no bounds and they were faced with a sometimes overwhelming barrage of questions.

She would spend many of the long summer days sitting on her swing, looking at her books and saying the words out loud over and over again until she was certain she had them right. Then suddenly she would break off and turn to her dolls. That was always a moment of pure joy for Jack and Ivy as they watched her play . . . just like any other little girl.

It was another of those things they had so long dreamed of and now it had come true. Her problems were disappearing like snow-flakes in the first flush of Spring. How long could it go on, they asked themselves. Now, and only now, they dared hope that within a few years complete normality would shine through and their problem child would only be a memory.

By now Ann had six dolls and without exception they were dressed as boys, but by some quirk she insisted that they have girls names. There was Julie, Phyllis and Angela, named after relatives, and there was Susan, Jane and Janet, named by Ann, after three of those children at the junior school who had become at the same time her helpers and her friends. What impression those children had made on that troubled little mind we will never really know. She never said. But in her handling of those strange boy-girl dolls there was a kind of affection that was hard to place. She loved them when she thought they were good, she sang to them in her fashion, and she scolded them when they were naughty.

Jack and Ivy couldn't help reflecting that whatever else their reward and punishment system had taught Ann, it had certainly shown her to know when others were being awkward!

Her insistence on dressing the dolls as boys had a bonus effect. Until then Ivy had made all the clothes for the dolls, but during the long break from school she encouraged Ann to keep up the needlecraft she had so painstakingly learned in class, and soon she was making jackets and trousers for the dolls.

She still didn't show any desire to mix with other children in the neighbourhood and appeared to be content to play in her own garden, and always at her side was Laddie. He wouldn't let anyone except Jack, Ivy, or the boys near her when she was outside. That most placid of animals would get up and walk in menacing circles round any stranger who came through the gate. The affection that had grown up between the two was at times uncanny. She would roll on him, sit on him, pull his ears and his tail and he would come back for more.

But more important there was an affection between Ann and her brothers that would brook no interference. Both Leonard and Leslie had grown into fine strapping boys—mad on sport, but not over-keen on school. Normal, healthy boys, in fact. They would join in any rough and tumble that was going, but with Ann they were gentle, loving and full of enthusiasm to show her the world that was so familiar to them, but completely new to her. They would gladly have died for her. They loved her deeply and they were, in their way, her protectors. Even when she wasn't there, as it turned out.

One day Leonard came home from school. It was obvious he had been fighting. His face was muddied and bloodied; his shirt was torn, with buttons missing. It took them a long time to get him to tell what had happened. They knew their Leonard. He was as tough as the next, but he didn't look for fights.

The answer was simple. It had been something that in a way they knew was inevitable. A boy had shouted: "Len Hodges has a sister who is daft." It was a remark that was instantly answered—with a smack in the eye.

They had been well matched for height and weight, those two boys, but Leonard had a passionate rage on his side. As he looked at his tousled son that evening Jack tried not to think too much about how the other boy must look. After all, Leonard had been the victor! He gave his sons a lecture about not fighting, but there wasn't a great deal of conviction in his voice. Leonard remembers that he didn't even get told off by Ivy for the tear in his shirt!

That remark was never repeated by anyone at his school. Too many had witnessed the results of a loose tongue.

When they talked about the incident that night Jack and Ivy could quite understand how it had come about. Ann still made those strange facial gestures and she still had her spasms of rage. They had been instantly accepted by those gentle children at her little school, but to perfectly normal children they must have appeared odd and a child out of the ordinary could quickly become an object for derision. Of all forms of cruelty, that perpetrated by child to child was undoubtedly the worst.

Soon it was nearing time for Ann to start at her new school and Ivy was beside herself with worry. No longer would she be able to accompany her daughter. A special bus would call, and pick her up. But far from being pleased at the end of the task that had lasted for four years, Ivy was filled with fear.

This was a step she had not expected and she knew in her own heart that it was a step that Ann was not yet ready to take. All these years they had watched over her, they had accompanied her everywhere. Perhaps in a way it was their fault, but they had kept her "wrapped in cotton wool," as Ivy put it. Whatever the reason, Ann still had no sense of danger, she could not understand traffic and had no idea of how to cross the road on her own.

Added to this was the problem of Ann's "peculiari-

ties." She pulled those dreadful faces, she had her
bouts of screaming—although they were becoming less
frequent—and she still laughed at nothing in particular. Ivy and Jack knew how cruel children could be
—what had happened at Leonard's school was an example—and they were sure that Ann could become
the butt of all the jokes on the bus.

But with all their hearts they wanted her to go to
the senior school, and if the only way she could go
was on that bus, then on the bus she would have to
go.

As it turned out, she didn't have to go on the bus
that first day. They were asked to accompany her and
have a talk with the headmaster.

The school was much larger than George Glover's
and extremely well-equipped. It catered for educationally sub-normal children from the age of eleven to
sixteen.

The headmaster had received a full report on Ann,
and he was sympathetic to the parents and full of
admiration for what had already been achieved. The
school was willing to play its part, he told Jack and
Ivy. If everything went well there was no reason why
Ann should not stay until she was sixteen.

But as they went home that day Jack and Ivy had
a feeling of foreboding. They had seen the hundreds
of boys and girls who had to receive attention at the
school and they were sure that here there could be
no question of Ann receiving the same help she had
from the other children at the junior school.

Then as the weeks passed, it appeared that their
fears had been groundless. Ann was settling down to
her lessons and they were told she was doing well.

But gradually it became apparent that she required much more individual attention than the hard-pressed teachers could give her.

They encouraged her to join in school activities like the choir and very gradually she did so. But if she was progressing in the class, out in the playground was a completely different, and for Jack and Ivy harrowing, matter.

In the hard process of growing up all children indulge in rough play. It was a way of releasing their pentup energies. But Ann, cocooned all those years by a loving, gentle family and protected at her previous school by those children who had taken her to their hearts, could not even begin to comprehend the rough and tumble—or the name-calling. Regularly she would arrive home minus her bonnet, or a glove or shoe. And then one day she came and sat saying over and over again "Nut-case, Ann," "Nut-case, Ann." It reduced Ivy to tears.

It had happened, as they feared it might, on that bus. A group of boys and girls who travelled with Ann had developed a game of what boiled down to baiting the idiot. They would make comments among themselves about the little girl and shout out names at her—and laugh. And that poor child with the sweet face would grin back at them. Not understanding. But if they were grinning then it must be funny. So in her innocent but overwhelming desire to be part of them she added to their delight by laughing at herself.

All this Jack discovered by painstaking questioning, and when he saw the picture for himself he was beside himself with rage. He went to see the headmaster, who was completely sympathetic, but pointed out that since it was happening outside school hours there was very little he could do about it.

It was to be the first of many visits and Jack was to reflect that the poor man must have become sick of the sight of him and fed-up with the many letters of complaint Jack wrote.

In a school that size it was physically impossible for the teachers to be watching Ann all the time. They were loving and patient with her when she was in the class, but she had to take her chance in the playground with the other children.

All the teachers did their best to make sure that she wasn't bullied, but, as in all schools when children find someone who doesn't retaliate to their taunts, they become outrageous.

Then the baiting went too far. Ann DID retaliate. It was vicious and violent, and in a way it was the beginning of the end of her stay at that school.

She couldn't distinguish between genuine jokes and real taunts so she lashed out, screaming and shouting. Then she would tear at her hair and her clothes and throw herself on the ground in fury until a teacher arrived to take her back to the class and try to calm her down.

She started to repeat swear words she heard from other children and would go round the house shouting curses at the top of her voice. Jack and Ivy were sick with grief and they kept her off school, and tried to carry on her education on their own. But they KNEW she needed proper schooling.

So they sent her back to school and for a few months things appeared to be normal, then the fighting would start again and the swearing. And Ann would retaliate. So they kept her off for another few weeks. So they limped through almost two years in this fashion.

Then the Medical Officer of Health sent Ann for an IQ test which proved a great success. There was no reason, he told the delighted parents, why her education should not continue. Her ability to learn was now growing almost as fast as her desire to learn. It was wonderful progress, and heartening news.

Then, as so often before, when they were buoyed up, the blow fell. The headmaster sent for them.

Ann would have to leave his school, he told them.

She was forging ahead with her reading, writing and arithmetic. She was taking an active part in cookery and sewing classes, but she was a hopeless failure when it came to social mixing. Her rages and weird spasms were having an adverse effect on the other children. He had to think of the majority and for that reason he had made up his mind that Ann should be excluded from the school.

In a way it was a relief. Jack and Ivy had known for a long time, indeed almost from the beginning, that it was not going to work out for Ann.

But what now?

There was silence for a few minutes, then the headmaster told them that he thought Ann would have to go to the occupation centre. They were stunned. Then Jack found his voice. He was outraged. Ann had proved long ago that she was educable, and everyone, even the headmaster himself, had agreed that she was doing well with her learning. She was NOT going to the occupation centre, no matter what happened.

Ann had fought for her place in life and it was not going to be taken away from her. The headmaster was slightly staggered by the passionate attack and told Jack that he would see what he could do. As it turned out he did wonders.

He phoned the couple two days later to say that Ann could have a home tutor. He had spoken to the Director of Education who had fully agreed.

What wonderful news. How he had done it, they didn't even pretend to know. But what they did realise, with a feeling of guilt, was that this man, like all the teachers, really had Ann's well-being at heart. It was probably for the best all round that she left the school. They would always be grateful to the headmaster for getting that home tutor.

Miss Ivy Evans came into their lives two days later and an immediate and lasting friendship developed that still exists today, even though Miss Evans retired before Ann was sixteen.

Ivy Evans was born in one of the Welsh mining valleys, but had moved North many years before. She specialised in teaching children who could not go to school—and she was an expert. Jack and Ivy never failed to marvel at her efficiency and her understanding of their daughter.

Ann became her devoted pupil. Their liking for each other was instantaneous and the progress that little girl made under the old woman's guidance was phenomenal. Miss Evans could only come two days a week—Tuesday and Thursday. She had other children to teach, but for Ann seven days would not have been enough. She quickly became obsessed with learning from Miss Evans and the subjects ranged from the three "Rs" to geography and general knowledge.

Before she left after each visit Miss Evans would set Ann homework, and insisted that it was completed before her next visit. In fact, it was always finished the following day. Learning filled all Ann's waking hours. How to spell words absorbed her and she would spend hours asking Jack and Ivy to spell this and that. Over the years, in fact, they found it helped them. Many of the words they had to look up in the dictionary!

They encouraged her all they could. The delight on her face made them feel humble and they were relieved to discover that the taunts, cruel pranks and swear words were soon forgotten.

They were also aware that she must have some recreation. From the day Miss Evans arrived Ann had spent less time on her swing and playing with her dolls. They decided they must do something about it, being only too keenly aware of what happened when it was "all work and no play."

They held another of their little councils of war and after a great deal of discussion they all agreed that it might be a good idea to buy her a scooter. It proved to be a resounding success.

Of course when she got it at first she hadn't a clue how to use it. But help from Leonard and Leslie and sheer determination soon gave her the hang of it. When she had a break from her lessons she would take the scooter out on the pavement and play happily for hours going up and down the pavement. They didn't have to worry about her safety. She was well protected by Laddie who trotted up and down beside her, brooking no interference from anyone. When he became tired he sat in the middle of the pavement, but never took his eyes off her.

By this time she was also obsessed by music and knew the words and tunes of all the pop songs and would spend hours humming the tunes, or singing the words, somewhat off-key. Then, quite unexpectedly, one day when they were out walking, Ann stopped and looked at a church. She asked if she could go inside and look. They took her in and explained as much as they could, and when they showed her the choir stalls she said she would like to be in the choir.

Both Jack and Ivy had been brought up as Anglicans, but over the years they had stopped going to church. It was just one of those things. Perhaps it was because most of their time had been taken up with looking after Ann. But since she had expressed a desire to join the choir they knew they must do something about it.

They contacted a friend and she was delighted at the idea and arranged for them to meet the vicar. That meeting was a dismal failure. It took place at a social evening and Ann went with Ivy. It could have been that she was overawed by the number of people there, or it may well have been her inability to mix socially, but she just sat beside Ivy and didn't speak. When Ivy asked the vicar if it would be possible for Ann to join the choir, he looked at Ann and simply said "No" and walked away. He didn't bother to explain further. Ivy, blinded by tears, took Ann's hand and walked out. She was enraged. After they had

come so far and received so much help from so many
people it hurt deeply that Ann had been rejected
by the church.

Over the years they have tried to reason the matter
out, but have never found a satisfactory explanation.
They knew there was a vacancy in the choir, so she
wasn't rejected because there was no room. They always reached the same conclusion. She was rejected
because she was different. They have never forgotten
that evening and it remains as a bitter memory.

As yet, of course, the rejection did not affect
Ann. They just told her that she could not join the
choir, and she accepted their word. The love and affection now being showered on their daughter by
their many friends went a long way towards helping
heal the wound they felt so deeply. It heartened them
to see their daughter responding, albeit only slightly,
to this show of affection from people other than her
own immediate family.

As Ann's education continued to bloom under Miss
Evans, the thirst for knowledge became a flood. All
the time it was questions. Where did this come from?
Where did that come from? She wanted to know
everything and again they found themselves hard-
pushed sometimes to find the right answer.

Then came the question that all children must ask
sometime. Jack opted out of that one and it was left
to Ivy to explain to her growing daughter the facts of
life and to prepare her for the moment she would
bloom into womanhood. Ivy took the task slowly over
the weeks until she was sure that Ann understood
everything she told her. Strangely, although Ann of-

ten repeated questions she had asked weeks before, that was one she never mentioned again.

Miss Evans was delighted with the progress her "star" pupil was making and was only too willing to agree when Ann asked for extra homework for the days she could not be with her.

When homework was finished she would concentrate on her sewing and within a few months she was making an expert job of everything she touched. She could hem a dress with such minute stitches that not one showed. And at long last she learned to tell the time. This was indeed a breakthrough.

For month after patient month they had tried to teach her, but they found they had to start by trying to explain the meaning of time. She just did not understand. It was no easy task, but gradually step-by-step they won through. Like so many things they had spent a long time teaching her, when she got the meaning of it she went on doing it as though it had never been a problem. In fact, telling the time became another of her obsessions. She told everyone the time, whether they wanted to know or not.

She still got these obsessions about many things and they developed a system of telling her when they were "good" or "silly." For example, telling the time, reading, writing and sewing were classed as "good," but measuring was "silly."

How that one came about they never really did know. There were so many things they could not understand about Ann, and never could. She would walk up to complete strangers and hold her arm against theirs to see which was the longest. Perhaps

it was a throw-back to the obsessions she had about
faces and legs, but it took a long time to cure. By
this time, of course, they were no longer using the
slapping and shaking method of getting her to do
what they wanted so she had to be broken of this
particular obsession by being scolded.

It was not until they had suffered months of em-
barrassment that she finally gave it up. It was as
though she had satisfied herself with what she had
been trying to find, and just switched off. Just like
that. One day she was out with Ivy and going through
the routine of measuring arms. The next day she
didn't do it, and in fact, never did it again.

Although they were delighted with her progress
they knew they had still a long way to go. An extremely long way. Ann was far from normal, but now
they accepted that and took everything as it came.

She had done so much in her life and there was
so much still to do. But they were determined not to
push her. She was fourteen and she had a lot of life
to live. Never mind, they told themselves, one day she
will catch up with it all.

She showed more emotion than most girls of her
age and there would be occasions when she would
walk out of a room and go upstairs. There they would
find her sitting on the bed cradling those strange
little boy-girl dolls and crying softly to herself, with
great tears running down her cheeks.

At those times they would gently comfort her and
talk to her until whatever had been troubling her
disappeared.

But out of all this emotion came the most marvellous moment of all. Ivy was sitting in a chair and

Ann walked into the room. Without a word she walked over to Ivy, put her arms round her neck and loved her as only a daughter can love her mother. It was the first time in her life that Ann had shown the affection that had for so long been bottled up inside her.

From that moment, as though a flood-gate had opened, she showered affection on all of them. Years of pain and heartbreak were forgotten. She had come out of the wilderness.

Ann had come home.

Goodbye to All That

Christmas that year was one of the happiest they could remember. For the first time in her life Ann took some part in the celebrations and they were sure that this time when they explained the Christmas story to her there was some form of understanding. They hadn't a lot of money to lavish on presents but what they did buy was carefully examined by Ann and her expressions of love for every gift, no matter how small, brought joy to their hearts.

Once unleashed that love knew no bounds. Her present to them on that Christmas Day was her delight, her laughter and the undying affection she lavished on them all.

Then soon it was her fifteenth birthday and on that day once again they took stock of Ann. The balance sheet of her life made wonderful reading. Her education had progressed beyond their wildest dreams, her talking was fluent and her questions gained in intelligence with every one she asked. She was for the main part reasonable and sensible and they hadn't experienced her rages for months. True, she was still inclined to cry a great deal at what appeared to be nothing at all, but they now knew it didn't do her any harm. In fact, they were convinced that these great shows of emotion in some way were helping her on the hard road to normality.

The most striking thing about her was her voice. It had deepened in tone, but she still spoke very softly. They didn't try to change it and today it is still one of the most attractive things about an extremely attractive girl.

When they looked at her on her fifteenth birthday they felt justified in the pride in their hearts. The only way for Ann now was forward. It appeared that all the let-downs and hurts of past years were behind them and they could now look to the future with pleasure.

Then, once again, a dark cloud drifted over their blue sky. All families have their ups and downs, but it appeared to Jack and Ivy that they were always being cast down just when they thought they had broken through to the top.

Ivy had been feeling unwell for some time, but tried to keep it to herself. Day after day she struggled on with her family, her housework and encouraging Ann with her lessons, but soon it was all getting too much for her, and she went to see the doctor. He sent her for hospital examinations, and a few days later he broke the news to her. She would have to go into hospital for a major operation. It was a dreadful blow to that little tight-knit community of a family, but much as Jack and the boys might miss her there was no telling what Ann's reactions would be. She loved them all, but was absolutely devoted to Ivy, lavishing all that love of those missing years on her. But she would have to be told.

So that evening Jack and Ivy sat with Ann and gently they explained to her as much as they thought necessary about Ivy's illness and about hospital. It wasn't so easy. They had to explain what a hospital was and what an operation was, but eventually they got it through to her that Ivy would be going away for quite a long time and that she would have to be a very good girl.

She eventually accepted all they said, and did not make a fuss, but she made Jack promise that he would take her every day to see Ivy. A few days before Ivy was due to go into hospital they took Ann on the bus and showed her where it was, and she appeared to be much happier about the situation after she had seen the building.

Jack's employers who had stood by him during all the heartbreaking years of struggle with Ann, now came to his aid once again. They told him to take as much time off as he needed. It was a marvellous gesture as he had been secretly fearful of leaving Ann on her own for long stretches at a time.

Then it was the day for Ivy to go into hospital. Jack managed to persuade Ann to stay at home. He knew a tearful scene at the hospital would not help any of them.

The boys were at school, so at the age of fifteen, Ann Hodges was on her own for the first time in her life. There had been so many firsts, but this was far different from any other she had encountered. Just before he left the house with Ivy, Jack looked at Ann and the ever-faithful Laddie at her side and he KNEW she would be safe. While that dog was there no possible harm could come to her.

But he didn't waste any time getting back from the hospital and there was a feeling of relief when he came in and found Ann sitting reading her schoolbooks. She had even set out her little folding work table. It was one of the days for a visit from Miss Evans. Her lessons filled Ann's mind for the rest of the afternoon, but when it was time to visit Ivy she was first to put her coat on. The first hospital visit passed without incident, for Jack and Ivy had earlier agreed to be as cheerful as they could when Ann was there. She was surprised to see Ivy in bed, and wanted to know why she hadn't had her operation that day. They explained to her that it would not be for a few days and she could come every evening with Jack until then.

Jack had to take on all the chores that Ivy had done with such practised ease for years . . . cleaning, cooking and washing and getting the boys ready for school in the morning. Like many men before, and since, he marvelled at the amount of work a housewife does!

The day before Ivy's operation he was washing shirts, and left them on the edge of the sink to go upstairs for some more things. When he came down the shirts had gone. He stared in amazement for a few minutes and then when he looked out of the window he saw Ann pegging them out on the line. Some were hanging by their tails, some by the sleeves and the rest had been pegged in the middle, but it didn't matter. Completely of her own accord Ann had done something she had seen her mother do so many times before. It was as though by some instinct she knew she was the woman of the house until Ivy came back to them.

After Ivy's operation Jack was told that only he could visit her. She was extremely ill and his visit could only be for a few minutes.

When he came back from the phone Jack realised he would have to tell Ann that she would not be able to visit Ivy that night. She was not downstairs and when he called her name there was no response. He ran upstairs and into her bedroom.

She was wedged in that little chair of so many years before, rocking back and forward with great tears running down her face and moaning. "Oh my Mummy," "Oh my Mummy." For some reason he would never fathom Ann KNEW that something was wrong with Ivy.

Gently he took her hands and pulled her from the chair and she put her arms round his neck and sobbed as though her heart would break.

For the next few days she was extremely quiet and hardly spoke to any of them. It was as though she had once again withdrawn into herself, but not quite like before. This time they knew the reason and they left her to do as she pleased. Then towards the end of the week Jack came back from hospital and his face was beaming. The operation had been a complete success and Ann could visit Ivy the very next evening.

On that visit Ann had something special to tell Ivy. It was something that would have to wait until Jack was out of earshot. She had become a woman. It had happened earlier that day. Jack thought she had gone upstairs to her bedroom to sit in the chair again and went after her, but she was in the toilet and told him: "Don't come in. This is for ladies only." She had gone to the drawer where Ivy had left everything prepared for her.

Jack knew what had happened, but waited to see what she would do. Ann made no mention of it to him and only told Ivy. They now knew that Ann could go through life keeping the secrets of womanhood to herself.

Ivy was in hospital for a month and every evening Jack, Ann and the boys visited her, keeping her up-to-date with all that had happened in their little world. Ann would sit by the side of Ivy's bed and hold her hand and gaze into her eyes. Sometimes she would be tearful, but they tried to ignore it and just let her sob quietly.

But most times she was bright and full of chatter, telling Ivy in great detail everything she had learned from Miss Evans. And so they struggled along until it was time for Ivy to come back. She had refused point-blank to take the offer of a month's convalescence in a home. She had been away from them for long enough, she said. She did not want to be parted from them again. The day before she came home, Jack and the boys went out of their way to make the house as clean and tidy as they could.

They all fussed over her, but none more than Ann. She followed Ivy everywhere. It was almost as though she thought if she let her out of her sight she would go away again.

Within a few days Ivy was taking over the chores again, but this time she had the most willing helper in the world. Ann desperately wanted to learn everything she could about housework. Until then she had not shown very much interest, and it gladdened Ivy's heart to realise that Ann's womanly instinct was at long last coming to the fore.

She started to teach her to use a sweeping brush and clean brasses and soon Ann was asking for more jobs to do. Always she wanted to do more. She was often clumsy, but Ivy never scolded her. She encouraged her all she could.

Jack realised that if Ivy was to get completely well she must get away from housework. She refused to go on her own, so there was nothing for it but to book a holiday. Once again they chose Blackpool. It held so many memories for them, and besides the air was good and bracing and it would be wonderful for Ivy. They couldn't afford an hotel or a boarding house, but they managed to rent a "do-it-yourself" flat and Jack and the boys took a firm line, saying they would do any chores that were necessary!

A friend took them by car and they were soon making themselves at home in the little flat—and staring out of the window at the driving rain. It was early in the year and the weather was cold, but after two days of rain a rather weak sun broke through, but it warmed the air a bit.

On that day the boys decided it was no holiday without having a dip in the sea so they went into their bedroom and put on their trunks under their clothes. Ann disappeared into her room for a few minutes and then they all went down to the beach.

As soon as they got on the sand the boys stripped off their clothes—and Ann did the same. She was wearing her bathing costume under her dress!

She ran down to the sea to join Leonard and Leslie and as soon as she reached them they started to splash her. Jack jumped up and ran towards them shouting with anger. Then he stopped. Ann was squealing with delight and trying to splash them back. He slowly retraced his steps to Ivy who was crying with sheer delight and together they sat on the sand and watched their teenage children larking about in the sea.

Not for the first time they thanked God for giving them such wonderful sons who knew Ann as well as they did and were doing all they could to treat her like a normal teenager. That incident had brought about another first for Ann. She had never worn her bathing costume in the sea before and after that day they spent the rest of the holiday watching her splash around as though she had been doing it all her life.

But as so often before, something was to happen to remind them that Ann still had a long way to go. The boys had gone off on their own and Ivy was buying groceries for the flat. Jack took Ann with him to the post office for some stamps. It was a large building with a revolving door and without thinking Jack went in, but as soon as she saw him being "swallowed up" a look of horror crossed Ann's face and she turned and ran blindly like a panic-stricken deer. Jack just turned in time to see her dashing along the pavement and went in pursuit.

Ann was a lot bigger than she had been all those years ago when she had dashed away after seeing the coach. She was tall and strong. Jack had very little chance of catching up. But this time she didn't run in a straight line, but went right round the block, and when he did catch up with her, she was almost outside the post office again.

With sweat streaming down his face and his heart pumping like a steam-hammer Jack had to lean against a wall in an effort to get his breath back, but he held Ann's hand as firmly as he could until he was able to speak.

He took her to the revolving door which had caused her so much panic and made her watch people going in and out and every few minutes he edged her closer to the door. Then he pushed her into it following her round and out again. The look of horror was replaced by sheer amazement. Why, she wanted to know, did some buildings have flat doors and others doors like that? Jack knew that he was in for a hard time. Revolving doors were put on some buildings so that people could come in and get out at the same time, he said. Why did buildings have doors anyway? she asked. Jack scratched his head. It was to stop the cold and burglars getting in, he told her. For the next hour he had to explain what a burglar was.

Once again it had been forcibly brought home to him that every strange word or happening had to be explained in great detail to Ann. Nothing could be taken for granted. There was so much she did not know or understand. There was so much she wanted desperately to learn.

It was something he was to ponder on for many weeks after that holiday incident, when they were back home in Salford. At fifteen and a half his daughter was a child of complete contrasts. She asked questions of such a high degree of intelligence that he was convinced that had circumstances been different she would have been university material. Then she would lapse into a form of baby talk and nonsense questions that were more in keeping with a four-year-old.

All her social activities were centred round her parents and her brothers. There was no youth club for her to go to. She did not have the ability to mix with "normal" teenagers. If only there had been a club for children like Ann it is possible that she would have blossomed forth much earlier. Children like her need to be sheltered and gradually allowed to mix with the outside world. At that time there was nothing. It was a great pity, but it was a fact and they would have to face the possibility of being her sole companions for the rest of her life.

Then Miss Evans told them that she would be retiring and Ann's tuition would be taken over by a younger teacher. They were heartbroken to see her go. She had become such a firm friend and a marvellous helper for Ann. With her, their daughter's education had leapt forward to a staggering degree. But they realised that Miss Evans had put in years of helping children who were unable to help themselves. She had earned her retirement manyfold.

The new teacher was young and eager and full of enthusiasm. She set to with a will to take over where the wonderful Miss Evans had left off and within a week or two she had won Ann's confidence and they became great friends. But it was not to be for long. The blow fell a few weeks before Ann's sixteenth birthday. It was contained in a letter from the Director of Education. As soon as Ann was sixteen, she would no longer be allowed a home tutor. He was sympathetic, but it was due to a grave shortage of teachers and there were so many handicapped children on the waiting list for home tutors and all of them had to be given the opportunity.

Jack wrote back and thanked the education department for all the facilities that Ann had received, and the help they had been given.

But in his heart he felt sore. Ann's education had

lasted just over nine years. In that time she had progressed from a hopeless, speechless, screaming walking vegetable to an attractive teenager who could read, write and spell as well as many normal children of her age. She had a thirst for knowledge that could not be quenched. Of all the cruel blows that had been struck in the name of bureaucracy, this was perhaps the worst. They were taking away the one thing she now needed most—formal education.

Certainly, they appreciated that there were other equally deserving children who required home tuition. They didn't question that. But they had fought for so long before they could even convince the authorities that Ann COULD be educated.

Now, when it was paying its highest dividend, that education was to be denied her.

Some rules are made to be broken. This one was not, and so the week after Ann's sixteenth birthday her formal education ended for good. They could not afford to have a paid tutor. If he had worked until he dropped—and he would gladly have done so—Jack would still have been unable to pay the fees.

It was a bitter pill to swallow, but it had to be done. Working without any outside help they had accomplished so much with Ann all those years before. They could do it again.

Or die in the attempt.

Homework and Housework

It wasn't to be an easy task. For one thing they were only too well aware of their own short-comings when it was a matter of the finer points of education. Both Jack and Ivy were of that generation who had had to leave school as soon as they could and go out to work to add to the meagre incomes of their own homes. But what they lacked in the way of formal education they more than compensated for with their natural intelligence.

Just because there was no longer any question of Ann receiving formal education they were not going to let the matter rest.

A few days after her sixteenth birthday when the home tutor was finally withdrawn, Jack and Ivy held another of their little councils with the boys and they discussed for hours what they were going to do.

Jack would take over the role of her "schoolteacher" and concentrate on the subjects she had so painstakingly learned and so desperately wanted to continue. He was a prolific reader and he knew in his heart that if he put his mind to it he would be able to keep pace with her insatiable desire for knowledge.

The boys for their part would continue to take her out with them whenever they could and point out all the things she had never seen but they took for granted.

Ivy decided that she could best serve Ann's education by really concentrating on her willingness to learn all she could about running a home. The enthusiasm for housework had started when Ivy was in hospital and had never waned. But they hadn't given her too much to do because they did not want to cut across her home lessons with the tutor.

Now was the time to channel that enthusiasm in the best way they could.

Ivy started by teaching her to use the thing she dreaded most in the house—the vacuum cleaner. A few years before, every time Ivy used the cleaner Ann would rush out of the room and hide until the machine was switched off. Now she had grown accustomed to its noise but she always regarded it with a great deal of caution and became very restless when Ivy was using it in the same room as she was in.

First Ivy took the machine to bits and showed Ann how to put it together. It took several days, but eventually she became adept at fitting all the nozzles and bits and pieces onto it, and in a way it became a sort of game. Then Ivy switched it on, and guiding Ann's hand made her push it back and forward over the floor. Like so many things before it became something of an obsession, and within a few weeks she would not let anyone else use the cleaner—not even Ivy!

She was meticulous in her use of it, vacuuming away every speck of dust, and her energy was boundless. She thought nothing of moving heavy furniture by herself to get at the carpet underneath. It warmed Ivy's heart to see her daughter being so painstaking. She had always been house-proud, and it was a wonderful feeling to realise that her daughter was being as particular as she was.

From cleaning Ann soon progressed to helping with washing and ironing, and soon became adept at both, and would spend ages getting every item she ironed just right, no matter how many there were.

Then, inevitably, she asked to learn to cook and Ivy decided she could start by making a pot of tea. For the next few days Ivy went over the process again and again until she thought Ann understood.

She eventually agreed that Ann could make a pot of tea one evening, but Ann insisted that they all leave the kitchen while she did so. "I'm not a baby," she told them.

When she appeared with her effort a few minutes later they all took a cup and as Ann stood anxiously watching, they sipped it. It was so thick and black, without milk or sugar, they could hardly swallow it— but swallow it they did, every drop. They told her she was a clever girl and hugged her and loved her. It was left to Ivy to explain to Ann that she mustn't put so much tea in the pot, and within a few days she was making perfect tea.

It was the same with everything she tried after that. If she did not get it right the first few times she would try and try again until she was satisfied it was exactly the way it should be.

The first meal she made on her own was roast beef, veg and chips. It was perfection, but Leonard and Lesile started to tease her about her cooking and walked away from the table, saying they were unable to eat the food. It was the first time they had really joked with her and they realised they had gone too far. Great tears welled up in Ann's eyes and she fled from the room to lie sobbing on her bed. Jack went into a towering rage and the boys, normally so sensitive to their sister's feelings, ran upstairs to her and comforted her.

They told her they were only joking, and as she dried her tears they found themselves having to explain the meaning of the word. They begged her to come downstairs with them and she could see how much they really enjoyed her cooking, and they would clear their plates.

Jack was still ruffled when they came downstairs and the sight of Ann's tear-stained face didn't help his temper. Ivy took Ann by the hand and told her to take no notice of the boys. She then had to explain what "no notice" meant.

Soon all was harmony again and at the end of the meal Leonard and Leslie couldn't have been louder in genuine praise of the meal. Those teenagers loved each other so much that they were soon the greatest of friends once again.

Later that evening when the boys went for a walk with Ann and the ever-faithful Laddie, Ivy amazed Jack by telling him she was delighted with the little episode over the meal. It was very simple, she said. Ann's reaction to the boys' remarks had been the reaction of any normal girl whose efforts at cooking had been criticised. Yes, Ivy said, she was well satisfied with the way things had gone.

But after that incident they were all very careful not to upset her and for many weeks afterwards, even when they praised her, she would ask them if they were joking.

Eventually, her obsession for housework and cleaning got out of hand. She wouldn't let Ivy do anything in the house and they had to gently apply some form of brake. They had to find something else to occupy her mind. Jack decided to teach her about money. It was something they had tried to teach her at school, but it had been beyond Ann's comprehension.

Jack got an assorted pile of pennies, threepenny pieces, sixpences and shillings and went back to the method he had used all those years before to teach her to count. He set them out in little piles on the table and night after night, week after week, he would show her how to count them out so that they made one pound. After weeks of tiring work the breakthrough came just when he felt he couldn't take any more.

Ann sat at the table with him and he scattered the coins. Without a word she sorted them out and made them up to twenty shillings. He varied the pattern, took some of the coins away, but she still counted them correctly. She hadn't learned parrot-fashion, and Jack was well-satisfied with his work. But a comment from Ann made him realise that there was definitely a right way and a wrong way to teach anyone.

"What is money used for?" she asked.

He had spent so long teaching Ann to count money that he had ignored the fact that she hadn't a clue what to do with it! As far as Ann was concerned she could have been counting different-sized beads, blocks or anything. They decided to make amends right away for this over-sight. That evening they carefully explained to her that when they got anything at a shop they had to give money for it and they told her that from the very next day when she went to the shops with Ivy she could hold the money and hand it over when they had made their purchases.

It was a very proud Ivy who set out the following day with Ann on this great new adventure. It was a huge success. She handed over the correct money each time and never once made a mistake, and even when she was given change she carefully counted it before putting it back in her purse. Soon she was demanding to go into the shops by herself so that she could not only pay for the goods, but ask for them as well.

Filled with anxiety at first they took to following her, but after a few days they realised that she never faltered and eventually they let her walk to the shops by herself. She had at last fully understood the meaning of money and, in fact, when Britain went decimal Ann was the first one in the family to master it.

There was only one cloud on the horizon now as far as Ann was concerned—the way she walked. Over the years she had developed the habit of plodding along, lifting each foot much higher off the ground than was necessary and firmly planting it on the pavement before taking the next step. It was something they had been unable to cure, and they had to admit that as she had grown, up, it had got slightly more pronounced. It broke Ivy's heart to see her thus. An extremely attractive teenage girl, who received more than her fair share of admiring glances when she was sitting on the bus, but caused sniggers among many girls her own age when they saw her walking. It was something they would have to concentrate on sometime, but they didn't really know how. They had told her off about it, but it had little effect. But if that was a problem, she was doing well at other things. Her climb up the ladder of life had been hard and long and they consoled themselves with the thought that if the only side-effect of her illness was an ungainly walk then they would be well-satisfied.

Ann was now seventeen and was at the age when girls of her age in the streets round about were going out with their friends, both boys and girls. They went to the cinema on their own, to dances and to cafés. Jack and Ivy were only too well aware that at seventeen many of these girls were already married with children of their own.

It was a serious and worrying problem for after all these years Ann wanted to be part of her own age group. She was no longer happy to be on her own. She wanted to belong, to mix-in and lead her own life as a normal young woman.

Most of her actions were now perfectly normal, but they knew she still had an extremely long way to go before she would be readily accepted by the outside world.

As a child she had lost so many years of the natural process of growing up. During those years, all her thinking had been done for her and although now she was thinking for herself there was so much she didn't know or understand. There was so much she still had to catch up on. It had taken years of patient love and understanding to get this far. It was probably going to take several more before they could allow her out into the world and not worry about her safety and her well-being.

Many of the questions she asked were still those of a child, and although they understood perfectly, it was impossible for strangers to comprehend the reasons behind the questions. She was so physically perfect that anyone overhearing her conversation on certain occasions would have found it laughable.

Indeed, that happened on many occasions. She was always willing to talk to strangers, but they for the most part became embarrassed at the childish quality of the questions and would either walk away or not bother to answer.

The reaction of the public was understandable, of course. Autism was still largely unknown to most, and although by that time a National Society had been formed in London it had received very little publicity.

Ann's housework was as perfect as it was methodical, and in the evenings she continued to concentrate on the homework set by the ever-patient Jack. He was now spending hours going round bookshops and the local libraries searching out books that would in any way help her education to advance.

What the future held for Ann they did not know, but it was becoming increasingly clear that the desire to break away from them, to be with people of her own age group, even for a few hours, had become an obsession. It was a natural progression from everything they had taught her, and they did not resent it in the least. In its way her desire to become part of the crowd was a marvellous step forward, and to stifle it could undo all they had worked for.

At last she was breaking open the hardest shell of all. She was beginning to cast out the devilment of autism from her mind. She had learned the meaning of sincerity and laughter and she loved them all.

The problem of finding someone of Ann's age to be her friend occupied most of their waking hours for months. It was beginning to be an insoluble task. They knew they couldn't go out and ask teenage girls to take an interest in Ann. It had to be someone who WANTED to be with her. The boys were marvellous in their way and took her out with them whenever they could, but they all knew that Ann was fretting to be with teenage girls and take part in the life they so obviously enjoyed. She had become very quiet and morose and it was obvious the lack of companionship troubled her deeply.

Then just as they despaired of solving the problem a young married woman who lived across from them called to see Ann. Kathy had five daughters of her own and had been preoccupied over the past few years in bringing them up, but now they were at school, she had time to concentrate on Ann. When the children were in bed she would visit Ann and talk to her for hours about teenage life, its perils and its pitfalls.

Within a few weeks they became great friends, the young mother and the teenage girl. Kathy was the answer to Ann's prayers. She talked to her like a sister and the little girls started to call her "Aunty Ann" and her delight knew no bounds. Kathy showed Ann how to put on make-up and she soon became an expert at it—although it became something of an obsession in the beginning!

With Kathy's help Ann started to find a new confidence and eventually went with her to a little shop she ran with her husband and helped serve the customers. What joy it was for her. She became a devoted "aunty" to the little girls and Jack thought his heart would burst with pride when he found that ANN was teaching the little girls to identify words and pictures in their books. Ann was teaching someone else!

If someone had told him ten years ago that she would be able to do that, he would have laughed in their face.

Now there was no doubt Ann was blossoming under that wonderful friendship, and soon her circle of friends grew. Kathy and her husband introduced her to other couples and they took her to their hearts. She went with them to the theatres and the cinema, to dances and clubs. They taught her the latest dance steps and she was a marvellous pupil, and soon became an expert dancer. But strangely it did not improve her walk. She still plodded along with that strange gait.

She danced round the house and her warm smile filled their hearts with sunshine.

By the time Ann was eighteen her determination to prove to Jack and Ivy that she would be a normal young woman was incredible. Spurred on by the help and advice from her new-found friends, her knowledge of the world outside was growing daily and her conversations were quite rational. Every day, it seemed to Jack, her questions were becoming more sophisticated.

At last that which she had desired most was coming to pass. She was taking part in the world about her.

Just how far she had progressed was demonstrated when Jack decided to re-decorate Ann's bedroom. She insisted on going with them and chose her own wallpaper and paint. But that wasn't enough. She demanded that Jack let her help him with the decorating, and after an hour's tuition she was painting like a professional. She helped paste the paper and hand it to Jack. By the Saturday morning when the room was almost complete, Jack realised that he would not have enough wallpaper. Ann begged to be allowed to go to the shop herself and get another roll.

Up to that day she had never travelled on a bus by herself, but she was so insistent that Jack and Ivy let her go.

It was only a short journey, but in a way it was one of the greatest moments of her life. However, after she had been gone an hour Jack could not contain his anxiety and went out to look for her.

He found her strolling along the road with the roll of paper tucked under her arm. She had walked home to save the bus fare!

From then on she was allowed to travel by herself on the bus whenever she wanted. But that wasn't enough for her and soon she became restless again. She saw all the young girls and boys of her age going to work and she wanted to get a job for herself.

Jack and Ivy knew that there was a limit to the

kind of work she would be able to do, but they didn't know of any firms who would willingly take on a girl who had been mentally ill the way Ann had been. It was a serious problem and they tried to explain it to her as best they could.

They told her that they didn't think she was ready for work yet, but if she waited a year or two they would get her a job. In the meantime, they told her, she must keep up her studies. The more she knew when it was time to go to work the better the job would be.

She accepted this explanation for a time and redoubled her efforts at learning. She read every book, newspaper and magazine she could find. She concentrated on her spelling until she was perfect.

But that only lasted until the day Leslie got a job at a local mill. Ann exploded with indignation. Why, she demanded, was her YOUNGER brother allowed to work and she was not? Jack and Ivy tried to explain as best they could, but found themselves faltering.

Ann kept up the question for days and was not in the least satisfied with the answers they gave her. Every day it was: "Why can't I go to work and earn my own wages?" until it became an obsession.

Now they knew they would have to explain fully to her what had been wrong with her. They told her about autism and that she had been ill from the day she was born. They explained that because of her illness she had lost many years of her childhood and that she had so much to catch up on and it would be impossible for her to work until she had caught up.

After the explanation was finished Ann sat quiet for a few minutes. Then in a puzzled voice she asked how one lost years when you couldn't even see them.

It almost stumped them, but eventually they told her that there was a period of time when she was young when she couldn't learn anything at all. She was now making up for that time, by learning now.

It took weeks of patient explanation to get the whole thing over to her and although she eventually accepted what they said, she did not agree that she was not ready for work.

So much so that one morning at 2 a.m. she walked into their bedroom and woke them up. When she was sure they were both listening she sat on the edge of the bed and told them that she could read as well as Leonard and Leslie, she could spell BETTER than them, she could cook, clean and sew, and go to the shops—things they couldn't do so well.

In many ways, Ann told her parents, she was better than her brothers. "I want to go to work when I am twenty-one," she said. They could do no other but agree with her. Satisfied that she had extracted that promise from them, Ann went off happily to bed, to leave her parents staring at each other in amazement.

She would not let them forget that promise and from that day threw herself into making plans for the great day when she would become a wage-earner.

Ann was going to get a job.

Helping Hands

That year autism was really brought to the attention of the public for the first time, with programmes about the illness on television and features in many newspapers. As it turned out they were to have far-reaching consequences for Jack, Ivy and Ann.

The *Manchester Evening News* carried a story about a little autistic boy and explained the problems his parents were having in bringing him up. When she read the story Ivy was so moved that she asked Jack to write to the parents that evening and tell them not to lose heart, and explain the success they had with Ann.

When she got that letter Jean Wynne didn't wait to write back. She phoned Ivy that day and during their long conversation Ivy explained all she could about Ann—and Ann talked to Jean on the phone.

What a marvellous moment that was. An autistic child speaking to the mother of another autistic, and with every word giving her new hope.

When the families met later that week Ivy could not hide her tears. Simon Wynne was just as Ann had been all those years before. An extremely attractive child, unable to speak or communicate. They talked for hours those two couples with so much in common and from that day they became firm friends.

As a result of that meeting Jack and Ivy decided to

join the local branch of the Society for Austistic Children. Norman and Jean Wynne were already members and worked tirelessly to get a better deal for children like Simon and Ann.

Ann attended all the meetings, helping to make the tea and hand round biscuits. Her very presence gave hope and encouragement to the parents when they realised how far she had come. "I am an autistic," she would say, "and I am determined to overcome my problems."

She was in great demand, and enjoyed every minute of it. She was gentle and loving with the children, and they in a strange way seemed to like her. There was a bond between them, an indefinable something. On many occasions she would be distressed by the fact that the children could not speak or communicate, but it certainly brought home to her how ill she had been all those years before, and it put to the back of her mind the burning desire to get a job.

She now understood so clearly why she had so much catching up to do but at the age of eighteen and a half she at last realised how far she had progressed.

Then Ann found herself in the news. The local paper, the *Salford City Reporter*, decided to carry a feature on the girl and her parents who had beaten autism and for hours Ann talked to writer Maureen Wood about her hopes and ambitions for the future —and the job she hoped to get. She had now made up her mind that she would work in an office and Jack and Ivy said that when they could afford it, they would buy Ann a typewriter.

The day after the story appeared, a young woman turned up at the Hodges' house. She was a secretary, she told them, and she wanted Ann to have her typewriter. They were overwhelmed, and didn't know what to say, but the young woman was firm. Ann was to have the typewriter and she had even brought paper and a rubber. As soon as the young woman had gone Ann sat down and started tapping out the alphabet, over and over again.

But that was only the beginning. A few days later a young man called to see Ann. His name was Peter Martin. He worked for a large office equipment manufacturing company and explained that the company gave electric typewriters to what they considered deserving charities. He thought that Ann should have one.

In the meantime, Peter said, he had business contacts who would loan her one and the very next day he turned up at the house again carrying the huge electric typewriter. Ann was overjoyed. Once it had been explained she found the machine extremely easy to use, and typing became an obsession. Every day she would sit in the little front room, tapping away at the keys.

Ivy phoned the young secretary who had so generously given her the first typewriter and explained the position to her. Would she like to have the typewriter back? But the young woman wouldn't hear of it. She asked Ivy to pass it on to someone who might be able to make use of it.

Not for the first time, they reflected on just how generous some people could be. For so many years they had been wrapped up in their own little family, because of Ann. Then when they thought she was being rejected they discovered that there were so many helping hands all around. People who had lived in the same area as them who knew nothing about Ann until they read it in the paper started to visit and they made many new and lasting friends.

And Peter Martin was by no means finished with Ann. A fortnight after he brought the typewriter, he turned up again, accompanied by two women. They were, he explained, expert typists and they wanted to see Ann for themselves. Even in a fortnight it had become obvious that Ann had a natural ability for typing, and they were deeply impressed by what she had done on her own.

They asked her if she would like to see round their office in Manchester, and Ann was so speechless with joy that she could only nod. The visit was fixed for the end of the week and for the next few days Ann could hardly sleep for excitement, and spent every minute she could at the typewriter.

When Ann arrived at the office her excitement was uncontrollable. She walked around for hours looking at the ultra-modern equipment and the expert girls who used it. She wanted to start work right away and had to be reminded that this was only a visit.

But she was so keen that it was agreed before she left that she could visit the office one day a fortnight and the girls would teach her how to file papers and do general office work.

On one point she was determined. It was arranged that one of the firm's cars would call to pick her up, but Ann refused. Office girls go to work by bus, she said. "I am going on the bus." There was no arguing about it. Her mind was made up.

It was wonderful news to take home to Jack and Ivy, but if they were not overjoyed it was not because they did not appreciate what was being done for Ann.

They had discussed what kind of work she should do over and over again, and they knew in their hearts that she was still not ready for office work. They knew that she would not be able to cope with the routine as a full-time job. They had to face the fact that Ann was still not fully normal. True, her progress was staggering. It amazed them when they realised just how fast she was learning. But facts had to be faced. They had wrapped her in a cocoon of their own making and Ann was struggling to get out and spread her wings. That was fine and they would help her all they could in that direction. But what Ann could not understand was that everything she did had to be taken a step at a time. It was how they had started with her all those years before and how they had progressed since.

Now nearing nineteen she wanted the process speeded up. Things were not happening fast enough for her and she could not understand Jack and Ivy's attitude.

In a way it was the classic situation of a teenager being at odds with her parents. A fairly normal happening, in fact. But in this case when Jack and Ivy said they knew what was best for her they were right.

They knew that now, perhaps more than ever before in her life, she needed their guidance and protection.

But they were at the same time overwhelmed by the help and advice she was receiving from people who only months before had been complete strangers.

She lived for the days when she could go to the Manchester office where she was taught to use a copying machine and improve her typing. She was shown, and quickly learned how to do routine filing jobs, and on the days she was at home she would pound away on that typewriter.

In fact, within six months she had become so much an expert that she could copy any written material given to her. But much as she enjoyed doing that she fretted to be at her "work" in the city.

On those mornings she would be up hours before anyone else and walked down to the centre of Salford to catch a bus into town. In the evenings she would make the same journey back.

And it was during one of those journeys that something happened that became an answer to another of their prayers.

As she left the office one evening Peter Martin, who had started it all, was behind her and that evening he phoned Ivy to say that he had been watching the way Ann walked and he was appalled at her gait. Ivy explained to him that they had been unable to do anything about it, but he said he could. He had an interest in a modelling agency and he wanted Ann to be allowed to go there for a course in deportment and make-up.

Ivy could hardly believe her ears. It just didn't seem

possible that all these things were happening. But happen they did.

The following Sunday Jack and Ivy took Ann to the modelling school, and it became a ritual. She was put on a diet to slim down her figure, she was tanght how to walk properly, and, as though by magic, she gave up her strange walk within weeks. She learned poise, and most important she at last learned the full meaning of social mixing.

The girls at the agency were marvellous. They were all trying to make their way in a hard, competitive world, yet they spent as much time as they could with the tall, shy, awkward girl and gave her confidence. Through them she learned a great deal of the outside world she had so longed to be part of. The lessons were never long enough for her. At home she would practise all the time and Jack and Ivy and the boys were amazed at the wonderful change in her. Even her speech had improved beyond their wildest dreams.

And so the months progressed and soon she was nineteen and a half. Peter invited her to attend the model agency daily and put her through the full course.

It was a moment of heart-bursting pride for Jack and Ivy the day they were invited to see her model her first dress, and her picture was featured in the evening paper. She had now, at long last, taken that first great step to the outside world by herself.

Her days were now filled with talk of being a model and then she would switch to wanting to help autistic children. She has never lost her compassion for those children who have been so cruelly afflicted as she herself was.

A few months before Ann's twentieth birthday Jack told Norman Wynne about the record he had kept of Ann's progress through the years. He had just finished copying them into a large ledger, and he asked Norman if he would like to read it in the hope that it might inspire Norman and Jean in their fight to find a place in the world for Simon.

Norman, a sports writer on the *Sunday People*, read it and the following week he brought it to me and asked me to read it.

As I read those simple jottings a remarkable story of a family emerged. I couldn't believe it was true. It just didn't seem possible that without outside help, or knowledge, they had virtually cured the incurable.

I had to meet them myself. And so, on a wet October day in 1971 I walked up the path to that house in Salford. It is a path I have walked many times since.

On that first day I was met at the door by Ann. Tall, blonde, extremely attractive, with a shy smile. Then there was Jack. A man of medium height, well-built, dark-haired and voluble. He talks wisely and knowingly of the world around him. He has in a way been blessed by this daughter. He has had the unique privilege of seeing the world and all its beauty a second time as he fought to make Ann see it too. They all have. Ivy, small and brown-haired with a warming smile. It was not hard to realise where Ann's looks come from. Ivy laughs a lot, but the laughter can quickly turn to tears as she goes back to the harrowing years and the struggles. Then there is Leonard. Slim and athletic, and Leslie, dark and rugged. In that house there is a great deal of love and affection. It abounds and overflows so that even a stranger feels welcome in their midst.

We talked for hours. The conversation was slow and hesitant at first. All of them shy about what had been accomplished, but not understanding that the outside world could be interested.

Then the words began to flow and as they talked they re-lived all those days of drama, the months and years of heart-breaking sorrow.

From that conversation emerged a story of love and devotion, the like of which I had never heard before. It was unfair of them to keep it to themselves. It belonged to every man to show that man can conquer every adversity. It belonged to those in despair and, above all, it belonged to all the Anns of the world and their parents. If only one of them was given hope by this story of devotion and over-riding love then the story must be told.

It is no easy task to ask a quite ordinary family to bare their innermost soul for strangers to see, perhaps criticise. Would perhaps the publicity have an adverse effect on Ann? There were serious and grave problems. They needed time to think and, as it turned out, held one of those little councils among themselves. In private. As a family. But this was different to all those that had gone before. For the first time Ann would take part in it. She would be asked if she wanted her story told. The decision would be hers, and hers alone. The answer a few days later was yes.

And so for me began a mammoth interview that became a labour of love and developed into a lasting friendship. It was a story I had to write. It became part of my life and gave me an insight into this scourging illness.

For Jack, Ivy, Leonard and Leslie, it meant going back to those days in the grim past and re-living them moment by moment. It was a lot to ask them to do, but they did it magnificently.

Out of it all came pure joy and laughter, and an unforgettable evening of high drama when we all learned secrets locked away in Ann's mind.

We were talking about her obsession for rocking in that little chair and how she would burst into laughter at nothing at all. Jack had just said that Ann, of course, didn't remember it, when Ann spoke: "I remember," she said softly. She was sitting on a couch with Ivy and after she spoke she went very quiet and leaned her head back and closed her eyes. The silence was unbearable. We all watched her, hardly daring to breathe. "I remember. There were teddy bears walking along the wall and dancing. They were so funny, I laughed and laughed."

She opened her eyes and smiled at us. We all spoke at once and fired questions at her, but it was no use. The spell had been broken. Then later that same evening the same thing happened again. She remembered why she went through that period of refusing to sit on chairs. The legs moved back and forward, she said. The chairs were not safe. And that plodding walk? Yes, she could remember that. That started because the pavements were sticky and she had to lift her feet high to stop them becoming stuck.

That was it. She could not tell us any more that night, and has not done since, of those days in the wilderness.

But if that was a moment of drama, her night at a cabaret was pure joy. Until then she had never stayed out after midnight unless she was with Jack and Ivy or her brothers. This was going to be different. No other member of the family would be there, only a group of friends and myself. A new dress was a must and she spent a day going round the boutiques to find just the right thing. New shoes and make-up were essential. But all these faded into insignificance beside the key to the front door. That was something she had not had before. Jack and Ivy had to promise they would not wait up. She must have her own key and let herself in—and they must be in bed!

That evening she dined and danced until the early hours. She clapped with sheer joy at the cabaret—and she captivated everyone who saw her.

Not for the first time I had to shake myself to remember that this was the same girl who had been written off only a few years before. The girl who had been given up for lost even before she had had a chance of life. How wrong the experts could be!

When she got home the house was in darkness. True to their word Jack and Ivy had gone to bed, although they were still awake. Ann ran upstairs and threw her arms round Ivy's neck and kissed her. From that moment she was allowed to keep her very own key to the door. She was nineteen.

A few weeks before Ann's story was due to appear, the *Sunday People* decided that she should take part in a commercial film for television to be shot in London. And so on a bitterly-cold December day Jack, Ivy and Ann travelled to London. Up to then Ann had never been any further than Blackpool. It was to be another great adventure. Another step forward. There were so many places and things she wanted to see. She knew so much about the city yet she had never seen it. Her energy was boundless. She was fascinated and captivated. She dined in Soho and she went to the theatre, and saw all the things she had read about.

The film was to be made on Wimbledon Common. A bleak and inhospitable place on a freezing day. For hour after grinding hour she obeyed the director as though she had been doing it all her life. Nothing was too much trouble for her. Long delays because of the bad weather were moments for joking and making friends with the camera crew and the so-numerous people needed for such a venture. But if the filming delighted her, she made her own mark on that highly-professional group.

They gave her a dinner at the end of it and presented her with a make-up bag—and they applauded her. Applause does not come easy from men who have had to deal with some of the great stars in the world.

And so back home to Salford, and once more to throw herself into the round of modelling classes, shopping and housework. All her days were now filled with sunshine—and dreams of far places and foreign lands. Geography had now become one of her great passions. Not an obsession. Obsessions had gone for ever.

She would spend hours looking at atlases and talk of all the countries she wanted to visit and jobs she wanted to do and the people she wanted to meet. She would spend hours talking of these ambitions. The desire to work at something full-time had now come back with a vengeance, but there were so many things to do before she was twenty-one. She was not yet twenty. There was another Christmas to look forward to, then her birthday and joy of joys, a holiday in Spain. In that land she had read so much about.

On her twentieth birthday she received dozens of cards, many from people who had never seen her, but had read about her. People who wanted to express their admiration for her and for Jack and Ivy.

But there was one card that day that will be treasured for all time to come. It was from Jack and Ivy. On it Jack had penned a little poem:

Oh angel dear,
The time has come
To enter the year before twenty-one,
We cherish the time that has gone before,
And remember the days and time of yore,
Our little girl has found at last,
The scourge of years at last are past,
And so we say,
Our angel dear,
Happy Birthday.

It is perhaps not the best poem in the world. But somehow it so movingly sums up the love and deep, undying affection by those parents for a child who through her illness and innocence had brought that little family so close together.

This story has no real end. Every day Ann learns something new and will go on doing so until, at long last, she has caught up with life. Her conversation is now completely rational. Thoughts of boyfriends, a husband and a home occupy her time. She loves children and has some very definite ideas on the subject of marriage. Her husband must be handsome and they will have two children—a boy and a girl. But above all her husband must love her and be a good father to the children.

Jack and Ivy now dare hope that someday in the not too distant future she will make a loving wife and mother. For them—and for Ann—it will be the crowning glory to a remarkable story.

It started all those years ago when a quite ordinary couple refused to accept that their daughter was incurable.

For the love of Ann they struggled to give her a life and the ability to find herself and the world and all its beauty.

They succeeded against all the odds.

Epilogue

On January 10, Ann Hodges was twenty-one. An age for celebration. A time to look to the future and its challenges. But for Jack and Ivy a time to look back and remember. So much had happened in those years from that day he was told he had a daughter. The first-day drama of the infant "turning blue with cold." Medical experts now believe that in fact at that moment Ann suffered a paroxysm of breathing. In those few vital seconds did she become autistic because of the shock to her brain? We will never know. It is a possibility. No more than that. But it is certain she did not "turn blue" with the cold.

Then to remember those first few months when the child showed the first signs of something being wrong and through that dreadful childhood to the day they were told that nothing could be done for her. If autism had been as widely recognised then as it is now, was it possible that the breakthrough with Ann would have come so much earlier? An almost unanswerable question, but one that Jack and Ivy often ask themselves.

But birthdays are times to think of happy days and moments of joy. There have been many of those in Ann's life. The marvellous moment of the breakthrough with her feeding, her counting and those first wonderful words. So many things and so many people to remember. People who have affected her life and given Jack and Ivy hope.

George Glover and his astounding teaching methods, Miss Ivy Evans, the family doctor, city councillors, neighbours, friends and casual acquaintances. So many of them who did so much and yet every one of them has found a place in that family's heart.

So much to remember, and so much to be thankful for. And so much to look forward to. Many years ago, Jack and Ivy were told that Ann would progress in seven-year cycles. It was true of the first seven years —when she learned to feed herself and progressed from there to her fourteenth birthday when she showed her first real sign of affection for her parents. The past seven years have exceeded their wildest dreams.

Their holiday in Spain last year was a resounding success and killed the last doubts they had about Ann's ability to take her place in the world.

The girl who only a few years before had fled at the sight of a bus, walked onto the jetliner like a seasoned traveller; the child who had become hysterical when she saw sea and sand, played on the beaches and splashed in the water. She who had shunned all human contact, accepted with laughter the many admiring glances from the young men. She joined in the fiestas and went to nightclubs, dancing until dawn.

And that strange child who created boys out of girl dolls, went shopping by herself in a a strange land for very special presents. She bought dolls for my daughters. Girl dolls, with long hair and flowing dresses.

Now comes the final step forward. Soon she will start looking in earnest for the job of her choice.

She will succeed.